Lester B. Brown, PhD
Editor

Two Spirit People: American Indian Lesbian Women and Gay Men

Pre-publication
REVIEWS,
COMMENTARIES,
EVALUATIONS . . .

"**T**his collection is a welcome contribution to the literature on sexual roles and identity within American Indian cultures. . . . It is a 'must read' for educators, social workers and other providers of social and mental health services."

Wynne DuBray
Professor
Division of Social Work
California State University

Two Spirit People: American Indian Lesbian Women and Gay Men

Two Spirit People: American Indian Lesbian Women and Gay Men

Lester B. Brown, PhD
Editor

Two Spirit People: American Indian Lesbian Women and Gay Men, edited by Lester B. Brown, was simultaneously issued by The Haworth Press, Inc., under the same title, as a special issue of the *Journal of Gay & Lesbian Social Services,* Volume 6, Number 2, 1997, James J. Kelly, Editor.

Harrington Park Press
An Imprint of
The Haworth Press, Inc.
New York • London

1-56023-089-4

Published by

Harrington Park Press, 10 Alice Street, Binghamton, NY 13904-1580 USA

Harrington Park Press is an imprint of The Haworth Press, Inc., 10 Alice Street, Binghamton, NY 13904-1580 USA.

Two Spirit People: American Indian Lesbian Women and Gay Men has also been published as *Journal of Gay & Lesbian Social Services*, Volume 6, Number 2 1997.

Cover art by Craig Cree Stone. Cover design by Marylouise E. Doyle.

Library of Congress Cataloging-in-Publication Data

Two spirit people : American Indian lesbian women and gay men / Lester B. Brown, editor.
     p. cm.
    Includes bibliographical references and index.
    ISBN 0-7890-0003-2 (alk. paper). -- ISBN 1-56023-089-4 (alk. paper)
    1. Indian gays–United States–Social conditions. 2. Indian lesbians–United States–Social conditions. 3. Indian gays–Services for–United States. 4. Indian lesbians–Services for–United States. 5. Gays–United States–Identity. 6. Lesbians–United States–Identity. 7. Indian gays–Diseases–United States. 8. AIDS (Disease)–United States–Prevention. 9. Social work with gays–United States. 10. Social work with lesbians–United States. I. Brown, Lester B.

E98.S48T84 1997
306.76'6'08997–dc21
                                97-3475
                                CIP

INDEXING & ABSTRACTING

Contributions to this publication are selectively indexed or abstracted in print, electronic, online, or CD-ROM version(s) of the reference tools and information services listed below. This list is current as of the copyright date of this publication. See the end of this section for additional notes.

- *AIDS Newsletter c/o CAB International/CAB ACCESS . . .* available in print, diskettes updated weekly, and on INTERNET. Providing full bibliographic listings, author affiliation, augmented keyword searching, CAB International, P.O. Box 100,Wallingford Oxon OX10 8DE, United Kingdom

- *Cambridge Scientific Abstracts, Risk Abstracts,* Environmental Routenet (accessed via INTERNET), 7200 Wisconsin Avenue #601, Bethesda, MD 20814

- *caredata CD: the social and community care database,* National Institute for Social Work, 5 Tavistock Place, London WC1H 9SS, England

- *CNPIEC Reference Guide: Chinese National Directory of Foreign Periodicals,* P.O. Box 88, Beijing, People's Republic of China

- *Digest of Neurology and Psychiatry,* The Institute of Living, 400 Washington Street, Hartford, CT 06106

- *ERIC Clearinghouse on Urban Education (ERIC/CUE),* Teachers College, Columbia University, Box 40, New York, NY 10027

- *Family Life Educator "Abstracts Section,"* ETR Associates, P.O. Box 1830, Santa Cruz, CA 95061-1830

- *Family Studies Database (online and CD/ROM),* National Information Services Corporation, 306 East Baltimore Pike, 2nd Floor, Media, PA 19063

- *HOMODOK/"Relevant" Bibliographic Database,* Documentation Centre for Gay & Lesbian Studies, University of Amsterdam (selective printed abstracts in "Homologie" and bibliographic computer databases covering cultural, historical, social and political aspects of gay & lesbian topics), c/o HOMODOK-ILGA Archive, O. Z. Achterburgwal 185, NL-1012 DK, Amsterdam, The Netherlands

(continued)

- *IBZ International Bibliography of Periodical Literature,* Zeller Verlag GmbH & Co., P.O.B. 1949, d-49009 Osnabruck, Germany

- *Index to Periodical Articles Related to Law,* University of Texas, 727 East 26th Street, Austin, TX 78705

- *INTERNET ACCESS (& additional networks) Bulletin Board for Libraries ("BUBL"), coverage of information resources on INTERNET, JANET, and other networks.*
  - JANET X.29: UK.AC.BATH.BUBL or 00006012101300
  - TELNET: BUBL.BATH.AC.UK or 138.38.32.45 login 'bubl'
  - Gopher: BUBL.BATH.AC.UK (138.32.32.45). Port 7070
  - World Wide Web: http: / / www.bubl.bath.ac.uk./BUBL/ home.html
  - NISSWAIS: telnetniss.ac. uk (for the NISS gateway)
  The Andersonian Library, Curran Building, 101 St. James Road, Glasgow G4 ONS, Scotland

- *Mental Health Abstracts (online through DIALOG),* IFI/Plenum Data Company, 3202 Kirkwood Highway, Wilmington, DE 19808

- *Referativnyi Zhurnal (Abstracts Journal of the Institute of Scientific Information of the Republic of Russia),* The Institute of Scientific Information, Baltijskaja ul., 14, Moscow A-219, Republic of Russia

- *Social Work Abstracts,* National Association of Social Workers, 750 First Street NW, 8th Floor, Washington, DC 20002

- *Sociological Abstracts (SA),* Sociological Abstracts, Inc., P.O. Box 22206, San Diego, CA 92192-0206

- *Studies on Women Abstracts,* Carfax Publishing Company, P.O. Box 25, Abingdon, Oxfordshire OX14 3UE, United Kingdom

- *Violence and Abuse Abstracts: A Review of Current Literature on Interpersonal Violence (VAA),* Sage Publications, Inc., 2455 Teller Road, Newbury Park, CA 91320

(continued)

SPECIAL BIBLIOGRAPHIC NOTES

related to special journal issues (separates)
and indexing/abstracting

❏ indexing/abstracting services in this list will also cover material in any "separate" that is co-published simultaneously with Haworth's special thematic journal issue or DocuSerial. Indexing/abstracting usually covers material at the article/chapter level.

❏ monographic co-editions are intended for either non-subscribers or libraries which intend to purchase a second copy for their circulating collections.

❏ monographic co-editions are reported to all jobbers/wholesalers/approval plans. The source journal is listed as the "series" to assist the prevention of duplicate purchasing in the same manner utilized for books-in-series.

❏ to facilitate user/access services all indexing/abstracting services are encouraged to utilize the co-indexing entry note indicated at the bottom of the first page of each article/chapter/contribution.

❏ this is intended to assist a library user of any reference tool (whether print, electronic, online, or CD-ROM) to locate the monographic version if the library has purchased this version but not a subscription to the source journal.

❏ individual articles/chapters in any Haworth publication are also available through the Haworth Document Delivery Services (HDDS).

CONTENTS

AIDS AND AMERICAN INDIANS

ABOUT THE EDITOR

Lester B. Brown, PhD, is Associate Professor, Department of Social Work and Department of American Indian Studies and Director, Department of American Indian Studies at California State University, Long Beach. He has also taught at Wayne State University, the University of Wisconsin-Milwaukee, and the State University of New York at Albany, where he was Chair of the Undergraduate Social Welfare Program for more than two years. Professor Brown serves as Advisory Board Member for the CSULB Multicultural Center and as an American Indian Studies representative. He is also Faculty Advisor to the American Indian Caucus of the Associated Students of Social Work. He has devoted much time and energy throughout his career to minority recruitment and retention at universities. Professor Brown has researched, written, and lectured extensively on this topic, as well as on AIDS and social work education, social work practice with minority groups, and sociocultural and service issues in working with people of color. He has been a member of the Council on Social Work Education and the National Association of Social Workers.

Foreword

Since the 1950s social work, along with its partners in the help-ing professions, psychology and psychiatry, has been seriously in-vested in studying the efficacy of its practices. Many practitioners in these professions came to appreciate that they must understand the culture and worldview of individuals if intervention is to be successful. Scholarly inquiries have made it clear that we must be familiar with the nuances of those who live around us. Brown et al., in this volume, have written articles that contribute to knowledge of important cultural areas that have not been the subject of previous scientific inquiry. They report cultural nuances that may help with effective interventions.

The articles in this collection explore a group of people in the United States not previously examined in any depth–American In-dian lesbian women and gay men. Many writers have told about First Americans, romanticized and studied them extensively. The Not-Men and Not-Women, discussed by Brown, have appeared in the literature, but not in the novel way Brown approaches them, as First Americans unique in their cultures and still very much a part of them. Occasionally these Not-Men and Not-Women have been touted as the first American lesbians and gays. But are they? Brown argues that they are unique gender alternatives, as are the lesbian and gay American Indians that were first mentioned in San Francis-co in the sixties. That these persons are unique and presently exist-ing poses problems for social work and other professionals. Can we see them as unique individuals without making their gender choices

---

[Haworth co-indexing entry note]: "Foreword." Epstein, Laura. Co-published simultaneously in *Journal of Gay & Lesbian Social Services* (The Haworth Press, Inc.) Vol. 6, No. 2, 1997, pp. xv-xvii; and: *Two Spirit People: American Indian Lesbian Women and Gay Men* (ed: Lester B. Brown) The Haworth Press, Inc., 1997, pp. xiii-xv; and: *Two Spirit People: American Indian Lesbian Women and Gay Men* (ed: Lester B. Brown) Harrington Park Press, an imprint of The Haworth Press, Inc., 1997, pp. xiii-xv. Single or multiple copies of this article are available for a fee from The Haworth Document Delivery Service [1-800-342-9678, 9:00 a.m. - 5:00 p.m. (EST) E-mail address: getinfo@haworth.com].

issues of pathology? If American Indian tribal groups can be accepting (and often extolling) of these individuals, can professionals be aware that these gender selections are not objects for therapeutic intervention?

The lesbian and gay American Indians described in this book are both American Indian and lesbians or gays. They look, sound, and lead lives that are similar to the rest of us. That they face many of the same issues as other doubly (and triply) oppressed peoples is not surprising. What the reports in this book help us see is that family and community acceptance of lesbians and gays is possible. American Indian cultures generally are models for other families and cultural groups, who are not so accepting of their lesbian and gay members. The families of American Indian lesbians and gays do not usually abandon or exorcise them, thus helping them face a generally unaccepting American milieu. Strengths gathered from accepting families can only be a positive aspect to their struggles to live.

Most therapeutic interventions are defined in Eurocentric terms, as if these were universal human attributes. Deviations tend to be deemed pathological. Inadequate attention has been given to differences in human behavior and development that are culturally or ethnically sensitive. Methods derived from that so-called universal base have been found to be deficient when used with oppressed groups. Such clients drop out of treatment or disregard therapeutic efforts in great numbers.

Although there is a demand for cultural and ethnic approaches, straightforward models for intervention do not exist. In earlier work Brown (with others) described necessary factors to accomplish ethnically and culturally sensitive professional intervention, particularly with oppressed groups such as American Indians and lesbians and gays. The works in this collection continue those efforts.

Recent efforts to demand that therapeutic endeavors work with clients who have differing cultural and worldviews have fallen on deafened ears, for the most part. The predominant therapeutic interventions ignore any such putative differences. Too often professionals see themselves as responsible for identifying problems that they attempt to change. We are all aware that attempts to change people who do not wish to change rarely work, and that the best opportunity for change to take place is in connection with problems that clients themselves identify and care about. Because many of the precepts of the therapeutic enterprise have become part of popular culture, the public often assumes that intervention efforts are successful. The therapeutic state, however, has done little to make life better for those trapped in its lower socioeconomic strata. Is it because the methods are lacking? Is it because we do not yet understand human nature enough to help people to change in ways they wish to change? Efforts to better understand oppressed groups should make it more possible to help them in the terms in which *they* request help. Brown and his associates have made an exceptional first effort at understanding a group of people who are previously unstudied. Social workers and other professionals who study them will benefit from these reports.

Laura Epstein, AM
Professor Emerita
School of Social Service Administration
University of Chicago

Preface:
Sharing the Gift of Sacred Being

And then the Great Spirit spoke
releasing two great whirlwinds upon the land
causing much death and destruction.
And we did not know which way to turn.
Then the Great Spirit whispered and all was silent.

–Farmer's Brother

Among many contemporary religiously conservative American Indians there is a belief that the Great Spirit put the Indians upon the earth for a specific reason. Accordingly, these conservatives believe that Native American religions, ceremonies, and worldviews must be continued, otherwise the world will be destroyed, both figuratively and physically. This belief is premised on the vision of a benevolent Great Spirit who has bestowed many gifts upon the Indian people. The gifts include, among other things, the physical environment, the human, plant, animal, and inanimate beings, as well as human institutions, ceremonies, and religions. In order to return gratitude for such gifts the Indian people show honor and respect in their daily lives and through ceremonies. Today many people look upon the sacred gifts bestowed upon the Indians as gifts for all of humanity. The environmental movement looks upon American Indian respect for and harmony with the environment as a

[Haworth co-indexing entry note]: "Preface: Sharing the Gift of Sacred Being." Champagne, Duane. Co-published simultaneously in *Journal of Gay & Lesbian Social Services* (The Haworth Press, Inc.) Vol. 6, No. 2, 1997, pp. xix-xxvi; and: *Two Spirit People: American Indian Lesbian Women and Gay Men* (ed: Lester B. Brown) The Haworth Press, Inc., 1997, pp. xvii-xxiv; and: *Two Spirit People: American Indian Lesbian Women and Gay Men* (ed: Lester B. Brown) Harrington Park Press, an imprint of The Haworth Press, Inc., 1997, pp. xvii-xxiv. Single or multiple copies of this article are available from The Haworth Document Delivery Service [1-800-342-9678, 9:00 a.m. - 5:00 p.m. (EST) E-mail address: getinfo@haworth.com].

model for the contemporary world. Other gifts include contributions to understanding democracy and community, and, perhaps most valuable of all, worldviews and religions that emphasize the sacredness of being.

THE SACRED TASK

It is documented in the academic literature that many American Indian cultures honored and respected alternative sexual lifestyles and gender roles. Some cultures are noted to have third or fourth gender statuses. Several papers in this volume reaffirm that traditional elders show great respect for Gay American Indians (GAI). I believe this view is consistent with most American Indian traditions and beliefs. Alternative gender roles were respected and honored, and believed to be part of the sacred web of life and society. If the Great Spirit chose to create alternative sexualities or gender roles, who was bold enough to oppose such power? In contrast, the Judeo-Christian tradition honors the male and female gender roles within the scope of heterosexuality, but alternative sexuality is regarded as sinful and outside of God's plan. Consequently, GAI have a much more benevolent and understanding tradition from which to assert their identity and reaffirm their sacred being. The Judeo-Christian tradition, and many other religions, deny that being, and lead to oppression and persecution.

GAIs are privileged in the sense that their religions traditionally reaffirm, respect, and honor their being. A viable and religiously informed Indian community should not oppress its GAI members. While this might sound idealistic and one might argue that such is not the case within many contemporary American Indian communities, there are many obvious reasons for this such as the acceptance of Judeo-Christian ethics among many tribal members, just to mention one. Nevertheless, the struggle for understanding and defining the status of GAIs is far from over, and holds great promise for reaffirming their traditional honored and respected role within Indian communities. Reaffirming a tradition of honor and respect is far easier than struggling against redefining and reinterpreting entire entrenched religions. The path to reaffirm the honor of GAI in contemporary Indian communities certainly will not be easy, but the cultural foundations are one of the sacred gifts of the Great Spirit, and therefore religion, tradition, and history are on the side of GAIs. Just as Indians are carriers of sacred gifts such as democracy and respect for the environment, Indian cultures emphasize the sacredness of alternative gender statuses and lifestyles, and this provides GAIs with a sacred purpose and plan. The gays and lesbians of other ethnic and cultural groups usually do not have access to similar worldviews emphasizing gay and lesbian identity and sacred status. The gift of sacred being is to be shared, and GAIs carry this gift for their brothers and sisters, and for the entire world.

The interpretation of contemporary American Indian religions that GAIs retain sacred rights within Indian cultures, and they can share this gift with others, have implications for therapy, identity formation, social movements, and general human relations. With the latter ends in view, some further interpretation may prove helpful.

The Sacredness of Being

In many American Indian worldviews, the universe is composed of beings of various power and purpose. All are to be honored and respected as part of the plan of the Great Spirit. Human beings, only a small part of creation, are not privy to the grand plan of the Great Spirit, but honor and respect must be to the given course of events, and humans must play out the role assigned to them as individuals and nations. Many ceremonies like Sun Dances, vision quests, and dreams are sought and interpreted for signs of individual and community purpose or wisdom. Individual vision quests or Sun Dances often are sought to gain knowledge of individual life quests. Dreams or visions gained in ceremony or during fasting can provide information about an individual's sacred life quest or role, or provide knowledge about the future of the community. Because an individual's life quest is gathered from sacred spirits, the revelation is regarded as personal and sacred. Much toleration of individualism in many Indian societies derives from the sacredness of an individual's personal mission in life. The ceremonies, power objects and spirit helpers revealed in the visions direct the person on a life task, which may only be revealed to the one individual, although often interpreted and guided by knowledgeable elders. Since many individuals have sacredly revealed missions, their activities, regardless of how strange they may seem to others, cannot be interfered with without retribution from the beings who are directing the sacred mission. Thus in many Indian nations, individualism is highly regarded, and each person may have a sacred mission in the world to perform as part of the great unknowable plan of the Great Spirit.

Therapy

By divine ordination, GAIs have a sacred mission to achieve as a group and as individuals. Many contemporary GAIs, like many other people of Indian descent, will have little knowledge about the manner in which traditional Indian communities honored and respected alternative sexuality and gender statuses. Most likely any therapist trying to help a GAI achieve positive self-esteem and identity will have little knowledge or wisdom about American Indian religions and cultures. Professional therapists can be trained to be sensitive to the concerns of GAIs, and the pages of this volume contribute to that understanding. Nevertheless, the wisdom and understanding that GAIs need must ultimately come from American Indian cultural communities. The wisdom to understand the sacredness of being from within one's own community, or from the cultural communities of other American Indians, can be gained most effectively through spiritual apprenticeship. Such apprenticeship is a lifelong commitment, but does not necessarily commit one to living in a rural Indian community. Much wisdom and knowledge could be gained this way, but it is not the only method to gain spiritual understanding. Professional therapists should be open to seeking the advice and help of Indian elders and spiritual leaders. Spiritual guidance and wisdom may be one aid to treating troubled GAIs. As time passes, however, members of the GAI community should seek their own interpretations of the sacredness of their being, and reconstruct their relations to Indian and non-Indian communities. Groups of spiritual GAIs could articulate the sacredness of GAI status, and work within Indian and non-Indian communities to reestablish proper forms of respect and honor. Such a path may not be easy, or even be blessed with wide appeal or acceptance, but it may have great effect upon improving individual views of self-worth, helping establish identity, and gaining respect and recognition. The world might not be changed, but the inner self may change, and that would be consistent with an Indian worldview.

Colonialism

One issue mentioned in this volume is the double and triple situations of oppression endured by GAIs. Not only do GAIs endure the oppression of their sexuality but also the minority status of Indians, while lesbians must also endure the oppression of their female gender. It is documented in this volume, and elsewhere, that the gay community has also discriminated against minority and ethnic group members. The general reaction among minorities, gays and lesbians, and GAIs is to describe, lament, and rail out against these multiple oppressions. This is surely an understandable response. To point out inequities and injustice is one method to seek understanding and redress. This reaction is a form of civil disobedience within the established body politic. All these possible remedies must surely be sought out and exhausted.

The multiple forms of oppression found in present-day society find their roots in the established sacredness of heterosexuality and gender relations. Such premises of defining alternative sexuality as profane provide few if any cultural resources for acceptance. For GAIs, the traditional worldviews carry an opposing valuation of the world, sexuality, and gender relations. Drawing on these traditions, GAIs can set forth a counter worldview to the current understandings of sexuality and gender roles. The Native traditions provide cultural resources for the reevaluation of sexuality and gender relations. Resistance to dominant gender valuations by itself does not set forth the establishment of positive identity and an alternative system of understanding gender relations and sexuality. Furthermore, an American Indian interpretation would not necessarily reject the multiple forms of oppression experienced by GAIs, since one possible interpretation of colonial domination is that the Great Spirit willed this, too. Therefore, following this line of reasoning, the spiritual warrior is not necessarily empowered to overthrow the present regime, but rather to find one's place within it, and to carry out one's sacred and creative life task within the context of the colonial regime. Since ultimately all being is becoming, the individual life tasks cannot but help transform the current state of human relations to a different, hopefully better, order.

The struggle with the current colonial regime and its multiple forms of oppression takes place in the realm of secular politics, but it can also take place in the struggle for defining values, ethics, morality, culture, and purpose. It is here that a GAI spiritual warrior may make a great contribution by accepting the challenge of a sacred task and life. By providing a living example to others, by seeking wisdom and knowledge about the sacredness of life and of Indian ethics, and incorporating those teachings into everyday contemporary life, the GAI spiritual warrior challenges the existing devaluation of alternative sexuality and understandings of gender roles. Rather than engage in negative reaction to existing legal, cultural, and political regimes, the GAI spiritual warrior might legitimately draw upon American Indian religions and traditions and constructively posit alternative valuations of gender and sexuality.

Tradition

When suggesting American Indian cultures and religious traditions as a source of inspiration and foundation for challenging the present-day valuations of alternative sexuality and gender roles, I am not suggesting a return to the religious and social life of several centuries ago. The colonial regime has made that impossible, and as noted above, the Great Spirit has set forth a new challenge, and that is preserving and sharing the sacred gifts of Indian cultures. It is not possible, genuine, or desirable to recreate the gender roles and sexuality honored and respected by past Indian cultures. Such recreations would be out of proper context, and most likely only imitate the former meaning and relations of former times and cultures. Certainly our continuous knowledge and appreciation can inspire the recreation of respect, honor, and sacredness of alternative sexual being, but this must be done for the present historical period, under present social, political, economic, and cultural conditions.

The sacredness of being teaches the honoring of the present world as a given sacred gift from the Great Spirit, and it is in this present-day world that spiritual warriors must achieve their sacred life tasks, for whatever purpose the Great Spirit wills. Attempting to recreate the past will only distract us from the future, where our spiritual tasks must have their contribution to the flow of human history. Therefore the reclaiming of the sacredness of GAI status must take place in the present historical, political and cultural situation. By taking on the understandings, beliefs, ethics, and wisdom of the Indian view of sacredness of being, the GAI can reaffirm their identity, worth, and purpose, and seek actively to recreate and contribute to a world that continues to hold them at arms length. While such rejection may continue for a long time, a GAI spiritual warrior, however, will not see that as a reason to reject and hide from the world, but will reaffirm the sacredness of the world, and seek to realize that sacredness within the inner self, within others, within Indian communities, within gay and lesbian communities, and throughout the world and present-day cultural and political relations.

A SACRED WAY

The examination of present-day Indian religious thought focusing on the sacred mission of Indian people to preserve and share the sacred gifts of the Great Spirit yields a possible path to greater self-esteem, greater cultural affirmation, and a guide to life and self-worth within a relatively hostile cultural and political climate. These beliefs can form a ground for GAI individual and group reaffirmation of purpose and have therapeutic value for individual GAIs in distress. Furthermore, this interpretation of American Indians as bearers of the Great Spirit's gifts also implies that GAIs have a responsibility to grant access to such knowledge and wisdom to gays and lesbians of other ethnic groups, whose traditions may not be so favorable as GAIs. In this way, the GAIs can share the gift of sacred being with other gays and lesbians, and with the heterosexual and Judeo-Christian worlds, within which Indian worldviews should also be honored and respected.

Brothers and Sisters a sacred way is before you.
All my relatives a sacred way is before you.
May the Great Spirit whisper soon.

Duane Champagne, PhD
Associate Professor and Director
American Indian Studies Center
University of California, Los Angeles

Introduction

After Columbus arrived accidently in North America, numerous interactions occurred between the indigenous peoples and those who followed Columbus here. These interactions ranged from friendly encounters to deadly ones. One friendly encounter introduced We-Wha, a Zuni tribe member, to representatives of the new government in Washington, DC. These representatives invited We-Wha to visit the Capitol. There We-Wha became the center of much societal activity. Attending many Washington parties and events, We-Wha, perceived as a multi-talented Zuni woman, met people ranging from the rank and file to the President. When she became ill, the attending physician discovered that We-Wha was biologically male. To the astonishment of the Zuni nation, We-Wha was shunned afterwards by the same people who had so extolled her talents before. European society could not accept this alternative gender person, probably the best known now of the not-women, about whom many articles and research reports have been written starting in the 1900s.

The alternative gender styles described in the first articles of this anthology explain in some detail who these not-men and not-women are in terms of American Indian gender alternatives. In the Identity section Brown explores the existence of not-men and not-women, persons of one biological sex assuming the identity in some form of the opposite sex. These identity transformations produced a third and fourth alternative gender style besides women and men. These not-men and not-women have been assumed by some to be progenitors of the present day lesbian and gay American Indians.

[Haworth co-indexing entry note]: "Introduction." Brown, Lester B.. Co-published simultaneously in *Journal of Gay & Lesbian Social Services* (The Haworth Press, Inc.) Vol. 6, No. 2, 1997, pp. 1-3; and: *Two Spirit People: American Indian Lesbian Women and Gay Men* (ed: Lester B. Brown) The Haworth Press, Inc., 1997, pp. 1-3; and: *Two Spirit People: American Indian Lesbian Women and Gay Men* (ed: Lester B. Brown) Harrington Park Press, an imprint of The Haworth Press, Inc., 1997, pp. 1-3. Single or multiple copies of this article are available for a fee from The Haworth Document Delivery Service [1-800-342-9678, 9:00 a.m. - 5:00 p.m. (EST) E-mail address: getinfo@haworth.com].

Brown argues that this is not the case; these not-men and not-women are alternative gender styles, as are American Indian lesbians and gays, who make up the fifth and sixth alternative gender styles in American Indian societies.

Little Crow et al. explore the ceremonies involved in which not-men and not-women chose to live as alternatives to those of the others in the tribe. The article also discusses how two tribes dealt with the existence of a not-woman, one rejecting and the other accepting the alternative lifestyle choices.

The article by Jacobs and Brown is an ethnographic study of present day American Indian lesbians and gays. By using in-depth interviewing, Jacobs and Brown have attempted to describe how present day American Indians who are lesbian or gay fit within American society and within their own Indian communities. What becomes obvious about those interviewed is that they are usually accepted by their families and the Indian communities but experience rejection and discrimination within American society. These lesbians and gays see themselves as accepted by their Indian communities, but do not see themselves as the not-men and not-women who continue to exist separately within Indian communities. Several of those interviewed mentioned attending meetings that have been held for the past few years. These meetings are held for Two Spirit People, those people who are North American Indian lesbians and gays from U.S.A., Canada, and Mexico. This gathering is a spiritual event held alternately in the U.S. and Canada, at which American Indians who are lesbian and gay can renew their spirituality in the midst of others like them.

The Social Services section contains two articles exploring the many issues that American Indian lesbians and gays experience. Walters has developed a detailed explication about their identity development. As part of this discussion she explains for practitioners the many issues confronting these individuals as they try to exist in two communities and societies: American and American Indian. The Wright et al. article traces social services issues for Indian lesbians and gays by reviewing the literature written by and about American Indian lesbians and gays. There are poetry, essays, and stories written by authors trying to understand and explore the meaning of being lesbian and gay and American Indian. Many of the issues faced by this group of persons have been explored in literature. Wright et al. draw out those issues of relevance to social service practitioners who may encounter American Indian lesbians and gays in their practice, particularly in urban areas.

The last section deals with AIDS and its impact on the American Indian community. Although not restricted to lesbians or gays in the Indian community, AIDS is having a distinct impact on them. The Rowell article presents the impact of AIDS on the Indian community from a national perspective. As Director of the National Native American AIDS Prevention Center, Rowell's article presents a comprehensive view of how AIDS is affecting the community and what is being done to help those at risk. DePoy and Bolduc also discuss the impact of AIDS; their article describes how one rural Indian community has tried to prevent HIV infection and the spread of AIDS.

The terms American Indian and Native American are used interchangeably in this volume. They are intended to mean the same, referring to the indigenous peoples of the continental United States. Both terms are, however, misleading. There are over 600 tribal groups living in this country. Each has its own culture, language, religion, and tribal and community customs. Using either term is simply a mechanism to make reading and understanding easier.

The papers in this compilation present perhaps the first known social science research exploration of the existence of lesbians and gays in the American Indian community. Earlier literature has examined not-men and not-women, and some authors have made the assumption that these were the first American Indian lesbian women and gay men. The material provided in these papers presents a different perspective and provides a beginning to understanding the place of lesbian and gay Indians within American Indian cultures and within American society. Hopefully, this beginning will prompt additional research and writing to help us understand these unique people and their places with us.

Lester B. Brown, PhD
Long Beach, CA

Women and Men,
Not-Men and Not-Women,
Lesbians and Gays:
American Indian
Gender Style Alternatives

Lester B. Brown

SUMMARY. American Indian tribal groups have a variety of customs unfamiliar to us. One particular occurrence is alternative gender styles for females and males. Gender has always been viewed as a spiritual calling and not determined by a person's anatomy. Some American Indians are spiritually directed to live as Not-Men and

Lester B. Brown, PhD, is Associate Professor, Department of Social Work and American Indian Studies, and Director, Department of American Indian Studies, California State University, Long Beach, 1250 Bellflower Boulevard, Long Beach, CA 90840-0902.

[Haworth co-indexing entry note]: "Women and Men, Not-Men and Not-Women, Lesbians and Gays: American Indian Gender Style Alternatives." Brown, Lester B. Co-published simultaneously in *Journal of Gay & Lesbian Social Services* (The Haworth Press, Inc.) Vol. 6, No. 2, 1997, pp. 5-20; and: *Two Spirit People: American Indian Lesbian Women and Gay Men* (ed: Lester B. Brown) The Haworth Press, Inc., 1997, pp. 5-20; and: *Two Spirit People: American Indian Lesbian Women and Gay Men* (ed: Lester B. Brown) Harrington Park Press, an imprint of The Haworth Press, Inc., 1997, pp. 5-20. Single or multiple copies of this article are available for a fee from The Haworth Document Delivery Service [1-800-342-9678, 9:00 a.m. - 5:00 p.m. (EST) E-mail address: getinfo@haworth.com].

Not-Women. These individuals lead lives unlike other women and men. Androgyny is an inadequate way to describe this occurrence. Explored in this article are the following issues: Who are these Not-Men and Not-Women? How were they viewed by the colonists? How are these alternative gender styles related to today's lesbian or gay American Indians? *[Article copies available for a fee from The Haworth Document Delivery Service: 1-800-342-9678. E-mail address: getinfo@haworth.com]*

INTRODUCTION

American Indian cultures and societies have had and many presently have a variety of ways in which gender is expressed. Social services professionals need to understand that gender has not always been defined in dichotomies: boy/girl, man/woman. American Indian groups have at least six alternative gender styles: women and men, not-men (biological women who assume some aspects of male roles) and not-women (biological men who assume some aspects of female roles), lesbians and gays. This paper will describe the not-men and not-women and discuss how they are related possibly to the more recent lesbians and gays, whom social workers may well encounter and with whom this volume primarily concerns itself.

Numerous articles and books have been written that attempt to detail the nature of American Indian cultures. One area that has received much attention is those women and men from numerous tribal groups who do not live day-to-day carrying out the usual female and male roles (Roscoe, 1991; Williams, 1992). These not-women and not-men seemed either to puzzle the newly arriving Europeans or in some cases the new immigrants were simply aghast and shocked by them. Many reporters have tried to define these unique American Indians, their customs and practices. A range of conclusions have been reached, with most centering around the idea that these not-women and not-men are a form of institutionalized homosexuality (Williams, 1992), i.e., the original lesbians and gays in this country (Katz, 1976). Although understandable as a conclusion, such a determination leaves much to be explained and also ignores much of the evidence about American Indians, their cultures and ways of behaving and interacting. Further exploration of the nature of American Indian gender styles is in order and may help clarify some of these issues.

The early accounts of immigrants to this country from Europe contain many references to the "hedonistic" nature of the way American Indians lived at that time (Angelino & Shedd, 1955). Most of these reports were written after 1700. In these writings newcomers failed to make an effort to understand and appreciate the new cultures they were encountering. In their haste to lay waste to the resources available in this hemisphere, they simply enslaved, killed or shunted aside any tribal groups that got in their way (Weeks, 1988). Those few newcomers who made efforts to observe what they encountered had mixed responses. However, most decided that American Indian groups needed civilization to save them.

Many of the newcomers to this hemisphere were from religious groups (Weeks, 1988). These clerics, of various kinds, and their strict followers very charitably proceeded to try to salvage the souls of American Indians. Although a number of behaviors bothered them, American Indian sexual practices proved to be most disturbing to their sensibilities (Roscoe, 1992). (It is important to remember how "puritanical" in nature were the Europeans of that time. Their reactions are understandable given their context, even though the aims, means and results of their actions are questionable in hindsight.)

American Indians had very simple beliefs about human sexuality and those beliefs were based on their experience. Briefly stated, sexual expression between women and men was essential for survival of the group; procreation was important. However, sexual expression was also fun and enjoyable irrespective of the partner's gender. As a consequence, adults engaged in sexual activities with persons of the same and different gender (Callender & Kochems, 1986). Sexual play was play, and no one could be harmed by it. Children, exploring sexual play as they still do today in most families in this country (American Indian and others), were not punished for trying something adults did in their spare time for pleasure (Crooks & Bauer, 1990). Children grew up and became adults with very few "hang-ups" about expressing themselves sexually.

For lack of a better or more appropriate term, bisexuality is used here to describe the nature of American Indian sexuality. (Polymorphous perverse sexuality [Webster's 3rd New International Dictionary, 1986] or pan sexuality [Ellis & Abarbanal, 1967] may also be appropriate or closer to the truth, but bisexuality is not necessarily misleading and is in more common use.) There were taboos about sexual play that could vary from one tribal group to another but they usually applied to all: Play with no one in your own family group. No sexual activity was to occur between not-men and not-women (which will be discussed later), and probably others that we don't now know.

In the latter part of the 19th century, researchers tried to label those European people who engaged in sexual practice for pleasure; they called them heterosexuals (Katz, 1976), or homosexuals if they enjoyed themselves sexually with others of the same gender. During this very conservative period anything sexual that was not for procreation was being studied and dissected probably to determine how to be rid of it, as opposed to simply knowing about it.

Efforts at studying and eradicating "deviant" sexual play have continued in this country since 1492. The proselytizing by religious groups convinced many American Indians to "mend" their ways to salvage their souls. Many American Indians simply nodded "yes" to everything and proceeded to act privately as they chose (Weeks, 1988). These latter individuals also tried to maintain as many of the traditional practices as they could. As a consequence, there is a tradition that has continued in several tribal groups that allows for gender styles that are the not-men or not-women. These persons don't fit the usual gender roles that women and men have played. That the tradition continues to exist speaks well of the strength and perseverance of American Indians and their cultures.

NOT-MEN AND NOT-WOMEN

One study within the past ten years (Roscoe, 1987) found over 200 different American Indian terms used by tribal groups to make reference to not-men and not-women. Some tribal groups had words for both; some only had a word or words for not-men or not-women but not both. There is no record of some eastern tribal groups having any words, although it is likely that they did. A brief mention in one early work refers to a Cherokee female-man (Roscoe, 1991). It is most likely that by the 1800s the eastern tribal groups had been so traumatized and beaten that gender alternatives were no longer permissible and in time their previous existence was not even a memory. Some mid-country and western groups did not suffer as long and as harshly as the eastern tribal groups. It is likely that many of their practices were altered significantly to "suit" the intruders, but they did not lose these alternative gender styles. They simply went underground and were not discussed with outsiders.

Not-men and not-women are described in numerous accounts although those by Williams (1992) and Roscoe (1991) are perhaps the most extensive and comprehensive. Here we will generally describe the nature of the not-men and not-women but caution the reader to go to more source material for details about these special people and for specifics about any tribal group. (For example, see Williams, 1992, and Roscoe, 1991.) The term "special" is used deliberately because most not-men and not-women were viewed as unique in most of their communities. Williams states this eloquently:

> Viewing things from outside the usual perspective they are able to achieve a creative and objective viewpoint that is seldom available to ordinary people. By the Indian view, someone who is different offers advantages to society precisely because she or he is freed from the restrictions of the usual. It is a different window from which to view the world. (Williams, 1992, p. 42)

Not-men and not-women are generally discovered to be different during childhood (Callender & Kochems, 1986; Little Crow et al., this volume; Roscoe, 1992; Williams, 1992). These differences are usually encouraged and nurtured. During adolescence these children would experience an initiation ceremony (described in more detail by Little Crow in this collection). For example, during the initiation ceremony, if they chose the other biological gender's implements, they were declared officially not-men and not-women.

All not-men and not-women had roles in their communities. Their roles frequently differed significantly from those of other women and men, but they had very definite places. A colleague once described this by referring to an American Indian table of organization—it has a place for everyone: No one is left out (Little Crow, 1993). Each tribal group varied in how these not-men and not-women functioned, but in most cases they were members of the community. They were rarely ostracized for being different, but if they were they could find another tribal group to accept them. More commonly they were revered and believed to have special powers, such as the gift of prophecy, because of their difference. They were called on frequently for exceptional service to their communities. They often served functions that no one else could do (Williams, 1992).

Not-men and not-women, although physically "normal," might best be described as not "fitting" the usual female or male persona. This non-fit might have to do with dressing differently, feeling differently, and/or behaving differently. One primary reason for the early attention to such differences is explained by the nature of American Indian spirituality. American Indians believe that each person is called on to play a part in the natural course of events. Most of us also lead lives like most others. Those who are very different, not-men and not-women for example, must have a special spiritual calling, based on the fact that they are called on to be different from others in the tribe and that they have special qualities and characteristics that differ significantly from others in the community (Williams, 1992).

Because of this special spiritual calling to be different from others, not-men and not-women were and are often viewed as having special powers. In some tribal groups they were assumed to be clairvoyant (Roscoe, 1992; Miller, 1982). In others, ceremonies could not be completed without the presence, leadership, and participation of the not-men and not-women (Williams, 1992; Callender & Kochems, 1986). They sometimes acted as go-betweens for matching up female/male couples (Williams, 1992). They sometimes were called on to give secret (private) names of great spiritual significance to children (Williams, 1992). There was an obvious economic benefit to having not-men and not-women present in tribal groups, because they were able to perform the usual female/male functions with greater vigor and industry. Not-men were reported to be exceptional warriors (Allen, 1981; Blackwood, 1984; Miller, 1982). Not-women were reported as being exceptional weavers and potters (Roscoe, 1992).

Most reports of not-men and not-women describe them in ways that make them seem to be some combination of female and male.

Androgenous, or as Callender and Kochems (1983 & 1986) describe them as "gender mixing," is perhaps the best word to describe their appearance. They neither looked totally like nor totally unlike their female or male counterparts. The expressions "neither woman nor man" or "not-men and not-women" seem to fit best and are used here. Some reports even speculated that the not-men and not-women were hermaphrodites, i.e., having the sexual organs and characteristics of both sexes (Williams, 1992). Such a being may have occurred in American Indian communities, as they do in most parts of the world, but none of the reports ever proved that this was true for the not-men and not-women. That no hermaphroditic American Indian ever has occurred is unlikely. However, not-men and not-women do not fall into this category.

Others have argued that these not-men and not-women are transgender persons. These reports argue that not-men and not-women were simply trapped in the wrong biological body, that they were really men trapped in women's bodies or women trapped in men's bodies. These suppositions leave unanswered the fact that these not-men and not-women are not reported to be dissatisfied with their bodies as are many gender dysphoric persons seen by psychotherapists today (see Little Crow et al., this volume, for more discussion of this issue). The reports of them imply or state that these not-men and not-women have a definite community role and that they perform that community role with diligence.

The many ways researchers have tried to explain these special people usually avoided the most obvious explanation: that these individuals were simply different and that they had preferences for dress, work, or behavior that deviated from the norms at the time. If the normative standards of a society don't proscribe the manner everyone is to follow, as does the most accepted and followed European model, then it is likely that some members of the society will be different.

When a society allows for any variation that may occur, there are likely to be some members who vary from the usual norm. In traditional American Indian societies, there are few proscriptions about the ways one chooses to live one's life. American Indian groups believe in an individual's right to individuality, to be different. In fact, individual uniqueness is more likely to be honored, as opposed to scorned as may occur in U.S. society.

Uniqueness in a person is more often than not believed to be a result of a special spiritual calling for the person in question, according to American Indian belief systems. As a consequence unique persons are more special and to be honored for this unique spiritual calling. That most not-men and not-women are unknown to most outsiders today is due to the fact that they would be viewed negatively or with curiosity by most U. S. citizens and, indeed, by many assimilated American Indians. The tabloids would probably have a field day reporting the occurrences of not-men and not-women. That not-men and not-women may and do still occur in American Indian cultures is a testament to the strength of American Indian groups and their belief systems.

One of the most famous not-women has been discussed in depth by Roscoe (1991). In his book the *Zuni Man-Woman,* Roscoe details the fascinating life of We-Wha, the most famous of the not-women that has been described in the literature. We-Wha lived a quiet life as a beloved member of the Zuni tribe. When discovered by European society, she was eventually taken to Washington, DC, where she enthralled members of high society. Invited to every important social function, We-Wha was very much in demand, *as an exceptional woman.* No one was aware that she was not biologically a female. Until this discovery even the President of the U.S. was taken by her charm and heaped praise on her for her accomplishments.

It is likely that tribal members were indeed pleased that the newcomers found one of their most special people to be as important as they did. Their chagrin would have been great when she was shunned after her biological status was discovered. However, today one can be quite bemused at the incredulity of the immigrant Europeans and then dismayed by their abject cruelty to one viewed as so important a member of a tribal community. It would not be unlike shunning a U.S. President's wife simply because her hair is really brown, not blond as it appears after being bleached. Does one's appearance determine the quality of the person? The adage of "One can't tell a book by its cover" didn't state or imply that if one is different from others' expectations that one is therefore not worthy of respect or admiration. One's appearance is simply a result of nature and one's own choice of style in appearance. It is not necessarily a reflection of anything else. The emergence in this century of a desirable androgenous "look" or style is an example of this. Although some (or many) may find it objectionable for themselves, there is no reason to dismiss the person using it. It is the way they look, not who they are.

Reports of specific instances rarely ever discuss not-men and not-women occurring at the same time, in the same place, and in the same tribe (Roscoe, 1987). Their occurrences are reported separately, although some tribes have words for both. Also, there are about ten times the number of reports about not-women than there are about not-men (Roscoe, 1986). This reporting discrepancy probably reflects a continuing European bias against women, in which cultures the roles of women are defined, determined, proscribed by men, and of generally little consequence otherwise, unless they deviate from acceptable norms. In those instances they were usually considered deviant and unacceptable. As a result of their devaluing women, Europeans paid little attention to American Indian women, but were quick to notice these "pretend" women, the not-women. Here we are not using the usual term to describe these not-men and not-women, since the word most frequently used—"berdache"—has a pejorative meaning (sodomite) and seems inappropriate to use in this cultural context. Derived from the Arabic and bastardized from Italian, then Spanish to French, the word was Anglicized and misspelled as well (Angelino & Shedd, 1955; Williams, 1992).

Sexual Expression by Not-Women and Not-Men

Most authors who have detailed accounts about not-men and not-women have drawn the conclusion that both are examples of institutional forms of homosexuality (Callender & Kochems, 1986; Katz, 1976; Roscoe, 1992; Williams, 1991). Although the accounts about not-men are fewer in number than those about not-women, most of the literature about not-men defines them as the first lesbians (Allen, 1981; Grahn, 1986). Several authors report "marriages" between not-men and other women (Allen, 1981; Blackwood, 1984; Schaeffer, 1965). Because "divorce" was relatively easy, there were always eligible women with children for these not-men to "marry" and then have children to raise as their own. Because gender did not determine sexuality, as is the proscribed case for European cultures, sexual expression between women and not-men was acceptable, just as sexual expression between women in general has been an acceptable means for experiencing pleasure in American Indian cultures (Allen, 1981). It is unfortunate that so much of the simple facts about not-men and not-women have been lost to time, probably primarily due to the oppressive and sexist nature of the immigrant Europeans who came here. That much about them is now not known is a great loss for us as human beings.

Not-women were reported to have taken other men as their mates (Landes, 1968; Lurie, 1953; Williams, 1992). That they did not commonly do so is not of any great surprise. As members in good standing of their tribal group, this was their right. As special people, they were very desirable as mates, as several authors have noted (Allen, 1981; Roscoe, 1992; Williams, 1992). Because they adopted the gender style of women, playing the part of a spouse to a man was a logical choice open to them. However, what is also reported is that, like not-men, they sometimes joined with "divorced" women who had children and raised the children as their own (Grahn, 1986). That they had sexual activity with both men and women is most likely. In that respect they were no different from all other American Indians, irrespective of their gender.

Bisexuality, as was mentioned earlier, was common for both women and men and that it was most likely the case for not-men and not-women as well is a reasonable conclusion. There is no reason that they would have fewer choices about their sexuality than other members of their societies. The only restriction placed on them seemed to be that they could not acceptably engage in sexual expression with other not-women and not-men. These individuals must be viewed as belonging to the same family of people for this incest taboo to occur. The literature is unclear on this issue.

LESBIAN AND GAY AMERICAN INDIANS

One has to question whether the sexuality expressed by not-men and not-women is a form of institutionalized homosexuality. Isn't it more likely, given the context of American Indian sexual expression, that these gender styles are equally as bisexual as other women and men? That they attach themselves to someone of the same biological gender for periods at a time doesn't mean their sexual orientation is exclusively homosexual. If they were homosexual, what did they become when they attached themselves to someone of the opposite biological sex? Can one so easily go from heterosexuality to homosexuality and back to heterosexuality, without simply being bisexual? Such switching is perhaps more common for a bisexual person than it is for a homosexual. If heterosexuality and homosexuality denote an affectional orientation above and beyond sexual expression, it can be argued that these not-men and not-women are most likely bisexual, that is, they have sexual and affectional preferences toward both other women and men. Some may have lived out their lives with someone of the same sex. Although none of the literature reports this explicitly, this could have occurred. If this was the case, one could argue that those specific persons were homosexual. However, most reports seem to imply that most women, men, not-men, and not-women enjoyed sexual expression irrespective of their partner's gender. Given this, bisexuality is a logical conclusion, if we have to label their sexual expression.

If not-men and not-women were and are bisexual, then who are lesbian and gay American Indians? The answer may be provided by the events that occurred in San Francisco in the 1960s. During the time that gay rights were being debated, a group appeared in San Francisco calling itself the Gay American Indians (GAI) (Roscoe, 1985). The organization of lesbian and gay American Indians has continued to this day and at least one other chapter of the organization was started in Minnesota. These brave American Indians began to assert their existence, as individuals and as lesbians and gays.

The literature about these lesbian and gay American Indians consists primarily of newspaper and magazine articles. Scholarly references believed them to be similar to, if not identical to, the not-men and not-women we have been discussing. Katz (1976) and others have referred to the not-men and not-women as the first American lesbians and gays. Tribal acceptance and sometimes emulation of the not-men and not-women was interpreted as the ultimate degree of cultural acceptance of the worth of lesbians and gays (Allen, 1981). American Indian cultures have been reported, and probably accurately so, as having no oppositional positions to same-sex sexual expression. The same belief is being asserted here and has been born out in the study about lesbian and gay American Indians reported later in this volume (Jacobs & Brown, this volume). American Indian cultures do not prohibit same sex activity, as has been mentioned earlier. The appearance of exclusively lesbian and gay American Indians may have more to do with the times than with any previously established tradition of homosexuality.

American Indians have historically been open-minded (for lack of a better description) about sexual expression. Procreation had been essential, however, if American Indian groups were to survive the encroachment of European influences. Being exclusively homosexual was always an option, but why would individuals limit their choices and risk the survival of the group? That kind of selfishness or self-centeredness would have been antithetical to American Indian cultures. Would it have been possible? Probably. Did it occur before the 60s? Possibly, but there is no record of such an occurrence, although many articles have expressed a belief that the not-men and not-women were homosexuals, transsexuals, transvestites, or hermaphrodites. Most of those interested in gay American history have argued that not-men and not-women's sexual expression was homosexual in nature and acceptable to the Indian communities. The American Indian acceptance of this homosexuality has been regarded as a model for all Americans to emulate (Katz, 1976; Williams, 1992).

Logically, one might assume that all of the above mentioned variations of sexual identity probably existed in American Indian communities to some degree. Difference, as has been noted, has always been highly prized in Indian communities, so such variations may well have occurred, although there is no mention in the surviving literature. Since difference is not necessarily a remarkable occurrence, or one calling for community rejection, there would be little reason to point out a "deviant." Such people would have a place in the community as does everyone else.

By the 1960s there seems to have been several events operating that may have contributed to increases in numbers of exclusively homosexual American Indians. Not-men and not-women, although continuing to exist, have been curiosities to Europeans; there have been extensive efforts to help American Indians to rid their communities of such deviants (Roscoe, 1987). Christian proselytizers have made so much fuss about the sexual "hedonism" among American Indians that their open and natural sexual expression has been either curtailed, eradicated or become hidden from prying non-Indian eyes (Allen, 1981).

Also about this time, the 1960s, a population growth of American Indians began occurring. For the first recorded time since Europeans arrived, the American Indian birthrate began to exceed the death-rate—American Indians might not be dying off after all. That exclusively lesbian and gay American Indians openly asserted themselves during this period of gay civil rights makes perfect sense. Their not-contributing to an increase in the American Indian population was not problematic, since the birthrate was up. Their acceptance in the traditional Indian community was a foregone conclusion. The rejection of a gay lifestyle by more assimilated American Indians was not problematic for them. The lifestyle might be rejected, but few American Indian families ever reject a family member simply because of difference. Difference of any kind is almost always acceptable in a family member. The open proclamation about the existence of lesbians and gays was not unlike the same assertion about the existence of African-American, Asian-American, and Latino-American lesbians and gays.

Gay American Indians (GAI) as an organization has continued to this day. Recently there have been efforts to get North American Indian lesbians and gays together yearly in order to build solidarity and to explore their American Indian cultures and spirituality as a group. These yearly gatherings here in this country or Canada have attracted hundreds of North American Indian lesbians and gays. Although those interviewed by Jacobs and Brown (this collection) reported their continued expression of American Indian spirituality and ways of life, these yearly gatherings are the first known attempts by lesbian and gay American Indians to immerse themselves as a group in American Indian culture and spirituality. Their freedom to do so says a lot about how the tolerance of difference, and even acceptance of difference, in North America may have increased. No one, however, is foolish enough to think that this tolerance is universal.

IMPLICATIONS FOR SOCIAL WORK PRACTICE

Not-men and not-women have a distinguished, if not fully understood or appreciated, history in American Indian cultures. Lesbian and gay American Indians also have, for at least the past thirty years or so, had an impact on the American Indian community and the U.S. They have shown that traditional American Indians have a wide-ranging and almost unlimited capacity to accept and even to encourage differences among their members. Differences of opinions and behaviors will exist, but rejection of a member by the traditional Indian community for differences is uncommon. The existence of lesbian and gay American Indians may or may not be a recent phenomenon, although the author has argued here that they are a recent occurrence. Their continued existence is likely. Their continued acceptance by their families and communities is a cultural phenomenon to be emulated. American Indian lesbians and gays continue to express themselves through Native traditions about spirituality and ways of living.

As these American Indians are encountered by social workers, it will be essential to be aware of their being both American Indian and lesbians or gays. They may express themselves in either culture, American Indian or American or a mixture of the two. These factors must be explored when they are clients in order to be sensitive to them as people and to the issues they bring up for assistance. Their lifestyles may vary considerably from those strictly American Indian or from those exclusively lesbian or gay. These variations are a part of who they are and how they live their lives. Knowing about American Indian cultures and about lesbian and gay lifestyles will help any social work practitioner to understand the nature of American Indians who are also lesbian or gay.

REFERENCES

Allen, P. G. (1981). Lesbians in American Indian cultures. *Conditions, 7*, 67-87.

Angelino, H., & Shedd, C. L. (1955). A note on berdache. *American Anthropologist, 57*, 121-126.

Beals, R. L. (1938). Remarks on the history of Pueblo social organization. *American Anthropologist, 40*, 340-341.

Bidney, D. (1938). Theoretical anthropology. *American Anthropologist, 40*, 712-713.

Blackwood, E. (1984). Sexuality and gender in certain Native American tribes: The case of cross-gender females. *Signs: Journal of Women in Culture and Society, 10* (11), 27-42.

Broch, H. B. (1977). A note on berdache among the Hare Indians of northwestern Canada. *The Western Canadian Journal of Anthropology, 7* (3), 95-101.

Callender, C., & Kochems, L. M. (1983). The North American berdache. *Current Anthropology, 24* (4), 443-470.

Callender, C., & Kochems, L. M. (1986). Men and not-men: Male gender-mixing statuses and homosexuality. *Journal of Homosexuality, 11,* 165-178.

Crooks, R., & Bauer, K. (1990). *Our sexuality, Fourth Edition.* Redwood City, CA: Benjamin/Cummings.

Devereux, G. (1937). Institutionalized homosexuality of the Mohave Indians. *Human Biology, 9* (1), 498-527.

Doran, D. C. *Preliminary findings of research regarding the sexual identities, attitudes & behaviors of Native American men who have (or have had) sex with other men residing in the eastern upper peninsula of Michigan.* Washington, DC: DHHS.

Ellis, A., & Abarbanal, A. (1967). *Sexual behavior.* NY: Hawthorne Books.

Fire, J., & Erdoes, R. (1972). *Lame Deer, seeker of visions.* NY: Simon and Schuster.

Fletcher, A. C., & La Flesche, F. (1911). *The Omaha Tribe.* Washington, DC: US Government Printing Office.

Gays in the U.S. (Wednesday, April 21, 1993). Long Beach, CA: *Press-Telegram.*

Gengle, D. (Jan. 28, 1976). Reclaiming the old new world: Gay was good with Native Americans. *The Advocate,* 40-41.

Grahn, J. (1986). Strange country this: Lesbianism and North American Indian tribes. *Another Mother Tongue: Gay Words, Gay Worlds.* Boston: Beacon, 43-57.

Greenberg, D. F. (1986). Why was the berdache ridiculed? *Journal of Homosexuality, 11,* 179-189.

Hay, H., & Burnside, J. (Summer 1979). Gay awareness and the first Americans. *RFD, 20,* 18-19.

Highwater, J. (1991). *Myth & sexuality.* NY: Penguin.

Hill, W. W. (1938). Note on the Pima berdache. *American Anthropologist, 40,* 338-340.

Hoebel, E. A. (1978). *The Cheyennes.* NY: Holt, Rinehart and Winston.

Jackson, P. A. (1989). *Male homosexuality in Thailand.* NY: Global Academic Publishers.

Katz, J. (1976). *Gay American history: Lesbians and Gay Men in the U.S.A.* NY: Crowell.

Kroeber, A. L. (1940). Psychosis or social sanction. *Character and Personality, 8*(3), 204-215.

Landes, R. (1968). *The Mystic Lake Sioux.* Madison, WI: The University of Wisconsin Press.

Landes, R. (1970). *The prairie Potawatomi.* Madison, WI: The University of Wisconsin Press.

Lurie, N. O. (1953). Winnebago berdache. *American Anthropologist, 55,* 708-711.

Miller, J. (1982). People, berdaches, and left-handed bears: Human variation in Native America. *Journal of Anthropological Research, 38* (3), 274-287.

Nanda, S. (1990). *Neither man nor woman.* Belmont, CA: Wadsworth Publishing Co.

Parsons, E. Clews. (1938). Brief communications. *American Anthropologist, 40,* 338.

Rebuilding through resistance: A Celebration of Indigenous Pride. (May, 1993). *The Lavender Network,* p. 1.

Roscoe, W. (Coordinating Editor) (1988). *Living the spirit: A gay American Indian anthology.* NY: St. Martin's Press.

Roscoe, W. (1991). *The Zuni man-woman.* Albuquerque, NM: University of New Mexico.

Roscoe, W. (1987). Bibliography of berdache and alternative gender roles among North American Indians. *Journal of Homosexuality, 14* (3/4), 81-171.

Roscoe, W. (Oct. 29, 1985). Gay American Indians: Creating an identity from past traditions. *The Advocate,* 45-49.

Schaeffer, C. E. (1965). The Kutenai female berdache: Courier guide, prophetess, and warrior. *Ethnohistory: The Bulletin of the Ohio Valley Historic Indian Conference, 12,* 193-236.

Spier, L. (1970). *Yuman tribes of the Gila River.* NY: Cooper Square Publishers.

Stevenson, M. C. (1905). *The Zuni Indians.* Washington, DC: US Government Printing Office.

Stewart, O. C. (Jan. 1960). Homosexuality among the American Indians and other native peoples of the world. *Mattachine Review, 6,* 9-15.

Stewart, O. C. (Feb. 1960). Homosexuality among American Indians and other native peoples of the world. *Mattachine Review, 6,* 13-19.

Stoller, R. J. (1976). Two feminized male American Indians. *Archives of Sexual Behavior, 5* (6), 529-538.

Thayer, J. S. (1980). The berdache of the northern plains: A socioreligious perspective. *Journal of Anthropological Research, 36,* 287-293.

Webster's 3rd new international dictionary. (1986). Springfield, MA: Merriam Webster.

Weeks, P. (1988). The American Indian experience: A profile: 1524 to the present. Arlington Heights, IL: Forum.

Williams, W. L. (1992). *The spirit and the flesh.* Boston: Beacon Press.

Gender Selection
in Two American Indian Tribes

Little Crow
Judy A. Wright
Lester B. Brown

SUMMARY. Providing social service assistance for ethnically diverse clients is perhaps one of the most challenging aspects of the social work profession. Academic and professional training often do little to prepare the social service professional for working with many minority groups, especially American Indians. This article provides insight into cultural norms concerning gender lifestyle choices among the Santee Dakota and Lakota tribes. This is followed by a discussion of the DSM IV classifications of gender dysphoria and transvestic fetishism, and how these labels may not necessarily apply to gay and lesbian American Indians. *[Article copies available for a fee from The Haworth Document Delivery Service: 1-800-342-9678. E-mail address: getinfo@haworth.com]*

Little Crow (a.k.a. Carl A. Bryant), is Director, The American Indian Unity Church, Garden Grove, CA. Judy A. Wright, BA, MA, is a Master's social work student, Department of Social Work, California State University, Long Beach. Lester B. Brown, PhD, is Associate Professor, Department of Social Work, California State University, Long Beach, 1250 Bellflower Boulevard, Long Beach, CA 90840.

[Haworth co-indexing entry note]: "Gender Selection in Two American Indian Tribes." Little Crow (Bryant, Carl A.), Judy A. Wright, and Lester B. Brown. Co-published simultaneously in *Journal of Gay & Lesbian Social Services* (The Haworth Press, Inc.) Vol. 6, No. 2, 1997, pp. 21-28; and: *Two Spirit People: American Indian Lesbian Women and Gay Men* (ed: Lester B. Brown) The Haworth Press, Inc., 1997, pp. 21-28; and: *Two Spirit People: American Indian Lesbian Women and Gay Men* (ed: Lester B. Brown) Harrington Park Press, an imprint of The Haworth Press, Inc., 1997, pp. 21-28. Single or multiple copies of this article are available for a fee from The Haworth Document Delivery Service [1-800-342-9678, 9:00 a.m. - 5:00 p.m. (EST) E-mail address: getinfo@haworth.com].

INTRODUCTION

American Indian cultures have provided and continue to provide a wide range of individual freedoms. One such freedom is the choice of gender, or more specifically, gender lifestyle. One of the more romanticized concepts associated with this cultural practice has been that the individual's gender choice need not be restricted to either male or female, but can be a combination of both. As we shall discover, however, this was and still is not the case among the Dakota and Lakota cultures.

The reader is encouraged to remember that there has always existed a great complexity of institutionalized social norms and mores among American Indian tribal groups despite the Europeans' practice of forming stereotypes which dissolved distinct cultural boundaries. The Lakota and Dakota tribes are used here to demonstrate the cultural diversity that exists even within a group that has generally been considered as homogeneous by mainstream U.S. society. From first-contact with Europeans, the Lakota and Dakota have been grouped together under the generic term of Sioux Indians.

The varieties of tribal worldviews that have survived despite homogenization of the Great Plains cultures have been instrumental in the formation and maintenance of a vast array of social norms that govern sexual identities and practices. There are also variances in what is considered sexually deviant.

TRIBAL PERSPECTIVES

Any ceremony (if, indeed it can be referred to as that) concerned with the rites of passage that involved matters of gender identification differed greatly between the Dakota and Lakota tribal groups. Perhaps the most notable difference involved how those individuals who opted for alternative lifestyles were treated by their respective tribes: one with regard, and the other with total disregard.

This article attempts to elucidate the wide range of social values adhered to by tribal people who essentially belong to the same language and cultural group. However, in reality, it can provide only a mere glimpse into this extremely complex subject.

The Dakota Santee

Among the Dakota Santee the "winkte" (the Dakota/Lakota term for Brown's Not-Woman, this volume) was assigned to a periphery social station within the formal kinship structure of the tribe. Ruth Landes (1968) describes the winkte's status as " . . . an inassimilable Dakota, a man who from earliest youth disliked hunting and war, and preferred the sedentary crafts of women."

Long before a young Dakota Santee came to make any conscious decisions about lifestyle preferences, he had been observed from infancy by peer and adult care-providers of the tribe. Therefore, all members of the group would know from early on when a boy was displaying patterns of behavior which demonstrated a preference for women's crafts and chores, rather than the standard activities considered common to young boys.

At some time during later childhood, the youth may have experienced dreams which were at times accompanied by visions. These spiritual events would either affirm or deny his early patterns of gender lifestyle practices. The dreams and visions that supported the youth's displayed gender traits were interpreted as Supernatural (higher entity) endorsement which granted him permission to practice the female arts. In most cases the gifts of dreams and visions bestowed upon the youth from the Supernatural also conferred certain powers upon him. In this instance, the winkte was considered to be a special type of tribal member, the Heyoka. Yet, even though he was assigned this special status, the Heyoka remained a marginal tribal member, never being afforded full acceptance and participation in mainstream tribal life.

Once this series of events had been experienced by a Dakota Santee youth, there followed what has been referred to as a tribal performance. Dakota taboos prevent relatives from killing one of their own family, therefore, these ceremonies were enacted to proclaim a social death of the individual. This performance served as a public declaration that a young man had chosen not to accept either the tribally defined male role or its assigned responsibilities. From this point on he was to be considered dead to all of his family members, both sanguine and fictive, and he could no longer interact socially with members of his tribe or family. Furthermore, to make it clear that he could no longer rely on a residential complex or village to provide material and physical support, the young man was banished from the camp or village where he had spent his childhood. There was no place in which to place this individual in the tribe's meticulously defined social structure.

The function of this performance was to maintain social equilibrium within the Dakota Santee tribal group. An individual who selected to follow the lifestyle of the winkte must experience total exile from his immediate tribe, and was abandoned to find acceptance and tolerance among strangers.

The Dakota did not include winkte in any formal or informal socially defined tribal hierarchy. This has been validated through both oral and documented Dakota Santee tradition. One would assume that with the passage of time, and the processes of cultural assimilation into dominant Western society, the attitudes and values concerning an individual's selection of alternative gender lifestyles would either have altered or vanished altogether. However, with few exceptions, apparent changes in tribal attitudes toward non-heterosexual gender identification among the Dakota Santee have, for the most part, been merely superficial.

The Lakota

In review of information pertaining to Lakota cultural practices, we immediately find a very different view of the winkte. One of the notable differences is their social involvement in the Lakota tribal community. These individuals were given a social classification that was exclusive to males who chose to live a non-heterosexual lifestyle. They were also referred to as winkte, but unlike the nonentity connotation inferred by the Dakota use of the term, the Lakota usage conveyed the meaning "would be woman."

Research done by William Powers (1986) has shown that the Lakota winkte were often referred to by the generic term, "wicasa wakan" or sacred man. These special men were classified into four major types based on their talents and abilities. The wicasa wakan were healers, performers, wizards, or winkte who assumed the female lifestyle, arts and crafts, and manner of attire.

Although the Lakota, similar to the Dakota, acknowledged Supernatural dispensation of the winkte lifestyle upon the individual, the Lakota tribes considered him an essential member of their society. Regarded as an esteemed member of their tribe, the Lakota winkte enjoyed prestige and high social status.

The divergence between Dakota and Lakota attitudes toward alternative gender lifestyles attests to the degree of diversity that existed (and still exists) among Native American tribes; even those considered to be of the same culture.

It appears that the winkte in Lakota culture played very important roles. An accurate list of their involvement and influences can only be imagined. But, we do know that they served as counsels to their tribes in matters of policy. They were sought out to name children, with such naming being seen as prestigious.

Unlike the Dakotas, the Lakota winktes took part in hunts, war parties, and for the most part, were the ones who took care of the old, feeble, and orphaned. Information derived from the Lakota oral tradition of transgenerational cultural transmission states that these individuals are included in the organizational hierarchy of tribal Male Ritual Specialists (Landes, 1968). Again, a sharp departure from the social amputation suffered by their Dakota counterparts.

There are many assumptions that can be made concerning these group differences. Perhaps one that stands above any other is the factor of assimilation (both cultural and religious) and the effect it has exerted upon these two distinct tribal groups. Noteworthy is the fact that historical treatment of individual freedom to select their own lifestyle in accord with their individual needs, has resulted in a greater degree of non-acceptance among other Native American tribes that do not allow such freedoms. Ironically, the adoption of dominant society's values which was originally intended to eradicate tribal religious traditions, has resulted in the perpetuation of the Dakota performance of exile and death for the winkte of both cultures.

IMPLICATIONS FOR SOCIAL WORK

There are two important factors social workers must be aware of when working with Native American clients. The first of these involves consideration of the relationship between Native American concepts (Dakota/Lakota, and other American Indian tribes) of alternative gender identity and the Western psychiatric concepts of gender identity disorders and gender dysphoria. No relationship exists between them.

The DSM IV (American Psychiatric Association, 1995, pp. xxiv-xxv) notes the expenditure of "special efforts to incorporate . . . three types of information specifically related to cultural consider-ations." However, when one turns to the section on Gender Identity Disorders (pp. 532-538), no subheading is found that addresses cultural factors which may affect the development of identity disor-ders or dysphoria. Diagnostic features of the disorder are described as including " . . . evidence of persistent discomfort about one's assigned sex or a sense of inappropriateness in the gender role of that sex . . . To make the diagnosis, there must be evidence of clinically significant distress or impairment in social, occupational, or other important areas of functioning" (Criterion D) (DSM IV, p. 533). One other definition, although not specified as gender identity dysphoria, dedicates one line (American Psychiatric Association, 1995, p. 538), item number 3 in 302.9, "Sexual Disorder Not Otherwise Speci-fied," which defines a sexual disturbance as a "persistent and marked distress about sexual orientation."

Given these guidelines, it is readily apparent that based on what has been presented in the first part of this article of the American Indian concepts of winkte, or Not-Man, Not-Woman (Brown, this volume), none qualifies as a gender identity disorder nor as a sexual disturbance. In American Indian tribes cultural accommodation was made, whether positive or negative, which allowed an individual broad latitude in making decisions as to gender identity. Even in the case of the Dakota Santee, the individual is not coerced or shamed into denying his chosen orientation. Although it may appear cruel to excommunicate the winkte from his home community, one must realize that a reasonable opportunity did exist for him to become accepted in a neighboring tribe that did not hold the same views as the Santee. There were rather extensive and sophisticated commu-nication and trade networks that linked tribal settlements across an area that ranged from Canada to the northern sector of Guatemala. These networks made it possible for any individual transient Indian to relocate to another settlement. (See Wright et al., this volume.)

Even in today's society, a large number of American Indians who have chosen to adopt alternative gender identities do not experience gender identity dysphoria as do their counterparts who are members of other ethnic groups. The social worker must allow American Indian individuals to define their own levels of functioning and satisfaction with their chosen gender identities, and not impose Western psychological labels upon them.

The second factor of Native American alternative gender practices that is of particular relevance for social workers is that of cross-dressing. Described as Transvestic Fetishism in the DSM IV (American Psychiatric Association, 1995, pp. 530-531), this disorder is characterized by the diagnostic criteria (302.3 on page 531) that include: recurrent, intense sexually arousing fantasies, sexual urges, or behaviors involving cross-dressing by a heterosexual male; and, fantasies, sexual urges, or behaviors which cause clinically significant distress or impairment in social, occupational, or other important areas of functioning. Expanding on this basic description, the DSM IV (p. 531) explains that in some individuals, the motivation for cross-dressing may change over time, temporarily or permanently, with sexual arousal in response to the cross-dressing diminishing or disappearing. In such instances, the cross-dressing becomes an antidote to anxiety or depression . . . in other individuals gender dysphoria becomes a fixed part of the clinical picture and is accompanied by the desire to dress and live permanently as a female and to seek hormonal or surgical reassignment.

Although this is an adequate psychological description of the development of cross-dressing within non-Indian culture, it is unrelated to the cross-dressing practiced by many who have chosen to live as winkte. Often when an American Indian male has chosen the Not-Woman lifestyle, he has done so in response to an elemental spiritual revelation which has validated his decision. He is in no way indulging in sexual fantasies, nor is his ultimate goal necessarily that of physiological transformation. Again, as in the case of gender identity dysphoria, the social worker must be aware of the Indian client's perspective of gender.

The discussion of these issues of gender identity should not be assumed to be applicable to every American Indian client one may encounter. There are many socialization factors that influence the quality of an Indian's psychological well-being with gender issues. In addition to the individual's tribal beliefs about these issues, one must take into consideration his primary and secondary familial and social support networks, the degree to which he has been assimilated into mainstream or urban society, and the specific personality characteristics he has chosen to display to the worker. Indian clients, with behavior that may seem to the social worker to indicate gender identity dysphoria, may in reality be assuming a culturally validated role. It is also possible that some Indian clients may truly desire sex reassignment surgery. However, it is hoped that this article has awakened an awareness among social workers that will prevent their culture-centric beliefs from precluding those of the American Indian client.

REFERENCES

American Psychiatric Association. (1995). *Diagnostic and statistical manual of mental disorders (4th ed.)*. Washington, DC: Author.
Landes, R. (1968). *The Mystic Lake Sioux: Sociology of Medwakanton Santee.* Madison, WI: The University of Wisconsin Press.
Powers, W. K. (1986). *Sacred language: The nature of supernatural discourse in Lakota.* Norman, OK: University of Oklahoma Press.

American Indian Lesbians and Gays:
An Exploratory Study

Mary Ann Jacobs
Lester B. Brown

SUMMARY. This article is a study of American Indian lesbians and gays. Using interview content, this study helps practitioners understand these virtually unstudied individuals. Interview data are compared to reports in the literature in an effort to understand how American Indian lesbians and gays are similar to and different from other lesbians and gays. Implications about future research and social work practice with American Indian lesbians and gays are discussed. *[Article copies available for a fee from The Haworth Document Delivery Service: 1-800-342-9678. E-mail address: getinfo@haworth.com]*

INTRODUCTION

Very little has been written about lesbian/gay American Indians. Any historical record of their existence in American Indian societies has been distorted by the priests, missionaries, and researchers who wrote about them. In some instances, their very existence has

---

Mary Ann Jacobs, MEd, is presently a PhD student at the University of Chicago School of Social Service Administration, 969 E. 60th Street, Chicago, IL 60637. Lester B. Brown, PhD, is Associate Professor, Department of Social Work, California State University, Long Beach.

[Haworth co-indexing entry note]: "American Indian Lesbians and Gays: An Exploratory Study." Jacobs, Mary Ann, and Lester B. Brown. Co-published simultaneously in *Journal of Gay & Lesbian Social Services* (The Haworth Press, Inc.) Vol. 6, No. 2, 1997, pp. 29-41; and: *Two Spirit People: American Indian Lesbian Women and Gay Men* (ed: Lester B. Brown) The Haworth Press, Inc., 1997, pp. 29-41; and: *Two Spirit People: American Indian Lesbian Women and Gay Men* (ed: Lester B. Brown) Harrington Park Press, an imprint of The Haworth Press, Inc., 1997, pp. 29-41. Single or multiple copies of this article are available for a fee from The Haworth Document Delivery Service [1-800-342-9678, 9:00 a.m. - 5:00 p.m. (EST) E-mail address: getinfo@haworth.com].

29

been completely covered up by Indian societies because of pressure from the dominant colonizing society and/or the adoption of Christian beliefs. Currently American Indian Studies interest in "not-men, not-women" persons has been revived (Allen, 1981; Roscoe, 1985; Williams, 1992). This exploratory study is ongoing. The initial group of participants were three women and five men. All of the participants are homosexuals living in several urban areas in California.

REVIEW OF THE LITERATURE

Most of the materials related to lesbian and gay American Indians are non-fiction literature, essays, and poetry. The few research reports that make reference to lesbian and gay American Indians do so in the context of the "not-women and not-men" discussed in Brown's article in this volume.

Recently, a study reported a non-random sample of 40,000 gay men and lesbians of whom 1.0% were gay American Indian men and 1.6% were lesbian American Indian women. The study looked at education, age, income, relationships and political involvement of gay and lesbian persons across the United States. The report states that a majority of the respondents held an undergraduate degree (31.5% of men and 32% of women); the median ages were 37 (men) and 35 (women); and that 4.3% of the men and 10.2% of the women had children under the age of 18. The average annual household income was $51,624 (for men) and $42,755 (for women) (*Press Telegram*, 1993).

Several newspaper articles appeared in the 1960s about Gay American Indians (GAI), then a newly formed gay organization in San Francisco. This was a period of gay liberation movement activity and GAI was actively involved in that movement. Like other gay groups formed by people of color, GAI actively tried to garner recognition of lesbian and gay American Indian rights.

Living the Spirit (Roscoe, 1988), an anthology of lesbian and gay American Indian authors, appeared in publication in the 1980s. Other literature by lesbian and gay American Indians was published during the 1970s and 1980s and is reviewed by Wright et al. in this volume.

Reports about lesbian and gay American Indians occurred frequently in the media during the period when the Gay American
Indian organization (GAI) was formed in San Francisco. This organization (continuously operating since the 1960s) still exists, although perhaps not as actively as during its formative years. More
recently, on a yearly basis, there is a North American convening of
lesbian and gay North American Indians for a multi-day event.
Alternating between the U. S. and Canada, this event is a gathering
centered in American Indian spirituality.

Scholars writing about "not-women and not-men" have frequently drawn the conclusion that these "not-women and not-men"
were this country's first lesbians and gays. Williams (1992), Roscoe
(1988), Allen (1981), and others have concluded that American
Indian lesbian women and gay men are these "not-men and not-
women" who have occurred among most if not all American Indian
tribal groups. We included in this study questions that would help us
to see if those people who self-identified as lesbian and gay also
saw themselves, or were perceived by their tribal communities, as
special people or as having special roles consistent with those reported about "not-women and not-men."

METHODOLOGY

In 1993 we interviewed lesbian and gay American Indians living
in California urban areas. Following a set of questions developed
for this study, each participant was asked numerous questions, most
allowing open-ended responses. (See Table 1.)

This group of American Indian lesbian/gay persons may or may
not be reflective of the larger American Indian lesbian/gay population. It was difficult to find American Indian persons who were
willing to identify themselves as homosexual and to discuss this
subject. We used personal contacts and also asked subjects for
referrals to find participants for this study. This study is currently
ongoing.

These interviews were very informal. Sometimes, the participants' answers were elaborate and in other cases brief. The participants were free to decline to answer any question(s) they chose. No
real names were used. The participants chose names they would

TABLE 1. Questions for American Indian Lesbian and Gay Interviews

1.   What name may I call you?

1a. Tell me about growing up, your family, etc.

2.   Your age?

3.   When did you first come out?

3a. Or, experience your first gay/lesbian encounter?

4.   Do you have a partner or lover?

4a. If yes, ask age, ethnicity, length of relationship and was the relationship monogamous?

4b. If no, have you had partners/lovers in the past? (If yes, describe them as above).

5.   In your gay/lesbian relationships, do you assume any particular kind of role?

5a. Is that role different from the way you enjoy relationships with others?

5b. What I'm trying to determine here, is, are you different in these (gay/lesbian) relationships? How?

6.   What has been the easiest part of being Native and a gay/lesbian man/woman?

7.   What has been the most difficult about being Native and a gay man?

8.   Who in your family knows about your homosexuality?

9.   What kinds of things do those that know you say about your homosexuality?

10. Who in your Native community knows about your homosexuality?

10a. What kinds of things do those that know you say about your homosexuality?

11. Is being a gay/lesbian man/woman made more difficult since there does not seem to be a Native gay/lesbian community?

11a. How would this have made life easier?

12. As a gay/lesbian man/woman, do you have any special place/role in the Native community?

12a. If yes, describe it for me.

13. Is the Native community accepting of gay and lesbian members?

TABLE 1 (continued)

13a. If so, how?

13b. To what do you attribute this attitude?

14. Are you familiar with the ways most articles have discussed homo-sexuality in the Native community?

14a. To what do you attribute the apparent change in attitudes historically?

15. What do you view as the biggest challenge for a gay or lesbian American Indian?

16. What is your tribal affiliation?

17. Are or have you been involved in the lesbian and gay community?

17a. If yes, how?

17b. If no, why not?

18. Have you regularly used drugs or alcohol?

19. What is the highest educational level you have achieved?

20. Do you have children?

20a. If so, do they know you are gay/lesbian?

20b. How do they feel about it?

21. Do you consider yourself a very spiritual person?

21a. How do you express your spirituality?

22. Do you belong to any organized religious group?

22a. If so, which?

23. What advice would you pass on to other gay/lesbian American Indians?

24. If you know of other gay/lesbian American Indian men/women, would you ask them to let me interview them? They can call me at 3------- to set up the interview.

25. What is your occupation?

25a. Household income?

26. Are there any questions you can think of that I haven't asked but should?

27. Is there anything else you would like to tell me about yourself?

28. Is there anything you would like to ask me?

like to be called for this survey. Each interview was taped and transcribed for use in this report. This survey has much too small a sample to draw any conclusions about the larger population of American Indian lesbians and gays. It may be useful for future larger studies which may be conducted within this population.

For this survey we were interested in finding out about some of the basic issues about being homosexual and being an American Indian person. We hoped to find out how American Indian lesbian women and gay men felt about being homosexual; how they were received among their families; and how the members of their American Indian communities responded to them as homosexuals and Natives. One of the tests of being homosexual is coming out to family and friends and we asked this group about that experience. The perceptions of the participants are interesting and may give some insight into the feelings of homosexual American Indian persons.

We attempted to look at a group that has never been studied systematically. Not being able to do a national study that would examine the population in depth, we proceeded to implement a local ethnographic study: to interview in depth a small sample of American Indian lesbians and gays. This report is the result of that study.

PORTRAITS OF THE RESPONDENTS

There were five male and three female participants. The median age of the women was 40.3; of the men, 34.4. One was a high school graduate; some had college work but less than a BA; two held a BA degree; two had PhDs; one did not respond. One woman and two men stated that they had children. A man and one of the women stated that their children knew they were/are homosexual; the other man did not have any contact with his children. A median income for this group is not reported here, because few respondents reported their annual income.

Most respondents identified their tribe(s) of origin. As can be gleaned from the following portraits, they have common themes as well as unique characteristics. The following portraits include a brief description of interviewees and a quote, chosen from their interviews.

Barbara (Lakota) is a woman, age 39. Barbara chose to live with her grandparents as a child because she said they were more traditional (than her mother). Barbara trains health care workers. She completed three years of art school. Barbara's first homosexual encounter was at age 17; her current relationship (of twelve years) is with an older white woman. They are raising her partner's son together. A quote: "Indian people are wholesale and invisible in this country . . . in our own country, and (this) is true in the Lesbian-Gay community. That is difficult . . . being invisible as Indian and lesbian."

Pat is a woman, age 42; no tribal affiliation was given. Pat has two children from an earlier marriage. Pat's first lesbian encounter was in high school (no age given) and her current relationship of five years is with a white woman. Pat has a BA and is an executive assistant in a national Native American AIDS organization. A quote: "I think the rudest awakening was when I came out of the closet and moved here 10 years ago . . . [that's] when I learned that the non-native community here of lesbians and gays is extremely racist . . . and not ready to deal with it. It was such a rude awakening; it broke my heart."

Lisa (Cherokee?) is a woman, age 40. Lisa is not sure that her tribal affiliation is correct. Lisa has an AA degree and is in her third year toward the completion of her BA. She had her first lesbian encounter at age 12; although involved in at least two long-term relationships (six months or more) Lisa is not currently involved with anyone. A quote: "If you are drinking or using drugs, try to get out of it . . . The best thing is to be spiritually connected. You can kind of look at the earth and see all these things that are happening that are negative. You need to walk through one day at a time. We are here for a purpose and keep moving."

Cherokee (Navajo) is a man, age 23; father of two children. At the time of this interview he was unemployed. Cherokee admits that he has been a hustler for many years. Cherokee had been living on the street for several years until recently when an American Indian family took him in. It is unknown what level of school he has completed. He had his first homosexual experience at age 15; at the time of this interview he had just ended a relationship with a lover he described as "Puerto Rican-French," age 21. A quote: "Out here in California it is hard to be religious cause you don't have the chief to teach you the way. I was just beginning to learn about the Dakota religion before I came to California."

Joe (Cherokee/Osage) is a man, age 40. Joe has a PhD and is an educator. Joe's first homosexual encounter was at puberty. By age 25 he was out to everyone. Although not in a relationship now, Joe has had several long-term relationships. Of his last three, he says his partners all contracted AIDS. He states that in the last two relationships both men knew they were infected prior to their relationship and did not tell him of their HIV status. Joe did not disclose his HIV status and HIV status is not a part of this study. Joe is very active in promoting gay and lesbian issues in education. A quote: "Make yourself known. Take pride in your accomplishments and positions. Celebrate yourself. Be a good role model."

Jim (Winabago) is a man, age 31. Jim has a BA and is employed as a grant writer and administrator. He had his first homosexual encounter at age 17. Jim's last long-term relationship ended a year and a half ago, when Jim's partner of eight years died. At the time of this interview, Jim stated that he was HIV positive. A quote: "The native way is that every day is how you express your spirituality and connection with a higher being and what your role is here. Stay in tune with that so that you are able to follow the wishes of the greater being and ultimately you are helping or giving something back by treating people decently . . . ."

Bill is a man, age 29 (no tribal affiliation given). Bill is the youngest child from a family of twelve. His mother died when Bill was young and he was raised by his father and siblings. Bill has completed three years of college and is still enrolled in school. He is currently in a training program with an AIDS foundation; Bill hopes this training will lead to employment. Bill came out at 21 and at the time of the interview was involved in a relationship with an older white man. A quote: "I don't look at myself as being native; I am just me . . . I don't have a problem with being gay . . . it is the other people who have a problem."

Red (Cherokee) is a man, age 49. Red is an educator with a PhD. His first sexual experiences were at fourteen, one with a woman and one with a man. He describes himself as a bisexual although most of his recent relationships were with men. Although Red is out to his family he does not choose to tell everyone in his community about his homosexuality, feeling "it is none of their business." Compared to the cultural stigmatization of homosexuality among other ethnic groups, Red believes that among many American Indian groups "there is no contradiction in being Indian and homosexual."

LESBIAN AND GAY THEMES

The participants (3 women–Barbara, Pat and Lisa and 5 men–Cherokee, Joe, Bill, Jim and Red) were asked a series of questions about their first homosexual encounter, their coming out experience, and their current relationship (if any). Most of the respondents stated that they had their first homosexual encounter between the ages of 12 and 21, or at the age when most persons are exploring their sexuality. Red stated that he is bisexual.

The coming out experience was very different for each. One woman stated that she never came out formally to family and that she and her family do not discuss sexual orientation or sexuality. One male stated that his family knows that he is gay; however, they do not discuss his homosexuality. All the others state that they are out to their families and at least some friends. Most reported that they came out as adults (18+). Only two males responded with their age at the time they came out; Joe came out at 25; Bill at 21. One woman (Pat) stated that when she came out her mother disowned her, but, then, when her sister came out as well, her mother began to communicate with her again.

When the study respondents discussed their current relationships, most expressed a desire/preference for a long-term monogamous relationship, even though some were not in those relationships at the time of this interview. All of the women had recent or current monogamous relationships with Caucasian women. Of the men, Jim and Bill each had monogamous relationships with Caucasian men. Cherokee was not in a relationship, but his last lover was of "Puerto Rican and French" (Caucasian) descent. Joe and Red did not describe a current relationship. Of all the respondents only Red stated that a previous homosexual relationship had been with an American Indian partner.

In many homosexual relationships partners may choose to "role play," that is, they assume a certain role or position within the relationship. In response to the query on playing a "role" only one male and one female identified as playing a role in their relationships. Most participants stated that they did not like playing roles and felt they were the same person in all their relationships.

All of the participants were out to their family members (for this study family was not defined; most participants responded to this question by including their extended families). They felt that their families accepted them as homosexuals, however, one individual noted a period of time when the family did not accept her homosexuality. As for being out in their American Indian community, only Red stated that not everyone knew and he had no desire to make his status a public issue. All of the participants felt that they (and their homosexuality) were accepted in the Indian community, with some holding activist positions with AIDS/HIV centers. The study participants agreed that the American Indian community in general was more accepting of their homosexuality than the general society, and that within the Indian communities the traditionalists were more accepting than were those with fundamentalist (Christian) values.

In some of the current literature about American Indians, it is noted that some American Indian societies reserved certain roles and responsibilities within the community for "not-women and not-men," described by some as the original American lesbians and gays. When the participants were asked if they felt there was a special role for them within their American Indian community (because they were homosexual), most respondents said no. Bill and Pat both expressed a desire and belief that they have a special role in being active about AIDS and HIV within their American Indian communities, but these roles were unlike any described in the literature about "not-women and not-men."

Among the group as a whole there was little familiarity of the literature about homosexuality in Native societies prior to the encounter with Europeans. Most responded that they believed that the negative attitudes in the American Indian community were a result or European/Christian ideals about homosexuality.

When asked what was the biggest challenge to American Indian lesbians and gays, the responses were all different. Barbara and Lisa both stated that being open about sexuality and accepting their sexual orientation was most important. Pat and Joe stated that AIDS and health issues were most important. Bill stated coming out to your family. Jim stated retaining our history and traditional values. Red stated maintaining self-esteem about cultural heritage and sexuality. Cherokee did not respond to this query.

None of the participants belonged to any organized religion, but most felt they were spiritual and expressed that in various ways. Lisa and Bill felt they expressed their spirituality through meditation. Joe, Jim, and Red felt that spirituality was expressed through their relationships with others. Barbara and Cherokee were exploring Lakota and the Dakota religions respectively. Pat participates in sweats and burns sage and prays. Again, none reported belonging to any formal religious group (Native or non-Native), but each felt these things they practiced in their daily living were an expression of their spirituality.

CONCLUSIONS

The participants for this survey all live in various urban areas in California. Their responses are sometimes reflective of that fact. The urban setting usually means that the tribal focus is less. Identifying as a member of the urban Indian community is more a matter of one's participation in group events such as Pow Wows or other gatherings. Some urban communities formed during relocation programs used by the Bureau of Indian Affairs (BIA) from the 1950-70s (Davis, 1994). Others are a result of a mixture of local tribes and non-California tribal peoples moving to an urban area for jobs and other opportunities. Our participants may have also relocated to an urban area because of their homosexuality, which is true of many other gay and lesbian people. Oftentimes on a reservation or in American Indian gatherings, the open expression of any form of sexuality is discouraged. This is increasingly the case since the advent of AIDS and HIV.

On the whole, this group of American Indian lesbians and gays did not appear to be very different from other lesbians and gays

(Brown & Oliver, 1986). A primary focus of this study was on their perception of acceptance by family and community. The participants in this study did report an open acceptance of their sexual orientation by both family and community. However, there are some instances in which the participants reported no discussion of their homosexuality with their family even though the family knew the respondent's homosexual status. Although this may seem curious, most literature on American Indian value systems (Sue, 1984) reports that open discussion of sexuality is discouraged.

While the "not-women, not-men" community status was not felt within this group, most reported some activist work related to American Indian lesbian and gay issues such as AIDS/HIV or to more general lesbian and gay rights issues. Although this study did not include questions about the participants' HIV status or their concerns about safe sex, most of the participants did talk about AIDS and HIV during the course of their interviews. Only one participant self-identified as HIV positive.

Lesbian and gay American Indians may have had a distinguished history, depending on one's reading of the literature about the "not-women and not-men." That lesbian and gay American Indians now exist is a certainty. That American Indian cultures provide a place for lesbian and gay members is apparent from the respondents in this study. That American Indian lesbians and gays have a place in their own communities helps make their lives easier in some respects. That they experience less familial pressures to be other than lesbian and gay is also a distinct advantage. That they still must encounter discrimination in American society for being lesbians and gays AND for being American Indian means they receive their share and more of oppression. That they continue to thrive and are so open is a testament to the sturdiness of American Indians.

REFERENCES

Allen, P. G. (1981). Lesbians in American Indian cultures. *Conditions, 7* (3), 67-87.

Anonymous. (Wednesday, April 21, 1993). Gays in the U.S. Long Beach, CA: *Press Telegram.*

Brown, L., & Oliver, J. (1987). *Sociocultural and service issues in working with gay and lesbian clients: A Resource Guide.* Albany, NY: Rockefeller College, State University of New York at Albany.

Davis, M. B. (1994). *Native America in the twentieth century: An encyclopedia.* NY: Garland Publishing, Inc.

Roscoe, W. (1987). Bibliography of berdache and alternative gender roles among North American Indians. *Journal of Homosexuality, 14* (3/4), 81-171.

Roscoe, W. (Coordinating Editor) (1988). *Living the spirit: A gay American Indian anthology.* New York, NY: St. Martin's Press.

Roscoe, W. (Oct. 29, 1985). Gay American Indians: Creating an identity from past traditions. *The Advocate,* pp. 45-49.

Roscoe, W. (1991). *The Zuni man-woman.* Albuquerque, NM: University of New Mexico.

Williams, W. L. (1992). *The spirit and the flesh.* Boston: Beacon Press.

SOCIAL SERVICES

Urban Lesbian
and Gay American Indian Identity:
Implications for Mental Health
Service Delivery

Karina L. Walters

SUMMARY. Research on American Indian identity has been, for the most part, poorly conceptualized and its findings contradictory. Indian identity has been shown to relate to positive mental health and cultural continuity and survival. However, the identity of gay and lesbian American Indians has not yet been addressed. Toward the formulation of a preliminary model of urban lesbian and gay American Indian (GAI) identity development, the author delineates acculturation levels, cultural

Karina L. Walters, MSW, PhD, is Assistant Professor, Columbia University School of Social Work.

Address correspondence to Karina L. Walters, Columbia University School of Social Work, 622 West 113th Street, New York, NY 10025. Electronic mail may be sent via Internet (kw81@columbia.edu).

[Haworth co-indexing entry note]: "Urban Lesbian and Gay American Indian Identity: Implications for Mental Health Service Delivery." Walters, Karina L. Co-published simultaneously in *Journal of Gay & Lesbian Social Services* (The Haworth Press, Inc.) Vol. 6, No. 2, 1997, pp. 43-65; and: *Two Spirit People: American Indian Lesbian Women and Gay Men* (ed: Lester B. Brown) The Haworth Press, Inc., 1997, pp. 43-65; and: *Two Spirit People: American Indian Lesbian Women and Gay Men* (ed: Lester B. Brown) Harrington Park Press, an imprint of The Haworth Press, Inc., 1997, pp. 43-65. Single or multiple copies of this article are available for a fee from The Haworth Document Delivery Service [1-800-342-9678, 9:00 a.m. - 5:00 p.m. (EST). E-mail address: getinfo@haworth.com].

43

values, and conflicts in allegiances that GAIs face in negotiating a positive identity. Implications for clinical practice, research, and mental health
service delivery are outlined. *[Article copies available for a fee from The
Haworth Document Delivery Service: 1-800-342-9678. E-mail address: getinfo
@haworth.com]*

The indigenous peoples of the United States are culturally heter-
ogeneous, consisting of more than 500 federally recognized and
200 non-federally recognized tribes. American Indians speak more
than 200 different languages, and over half live in urban cities (U.S.
Bureau of the Census, 1994). Despite the ubiquitousness of lesbian
and gay American Indians (GAIs), who can be found in rural,
reservation, and city environments, mental health researchers have
historically ignored them.

Gay and lesbian identity and ethnic identity are integrally connected to psychological well-being (Jones, 1991; Phinney, 1990;
Sue, 1992; Walters & Simoni, 1993) and are important variables to
consider in the provision of culturally sensitive clinical treatment
(Jones, 1991; Morales, 1989; Phinney, 1990; Trimble, 1981). How
GAIs cope with the stress associated with negotiating their gay and
lesbian identity and their Indian ethnic identity has direct effects on
their mental health functioning (Jarvenpa, 1985; Kemnitzer, 1978).
No studies on gay and lesbian American Indian identity currently
exist. Accordingly, mental health research remains inadequate in
providing any social service guidelines that can incorporate GAI
identity issues. Understanding GAI identity development will assist
social service providers in imparting culturally relevant services.
Additionally, it will assist social service researchers in understanding other Indian client behaviors such as mental health service
utilization, psychosocial adaptation, self-esteem development, and
counselor preference (Atkinson, Morten, & Sue, 1983; LaFromboise, 1988; Sue & Sue, 1990; Sue, 1992). Given the evidence that
identity is a critical variable for both ethnic and gay individuals,
variables associated with American Indian gay and lesbian identity
development merit further study. As a first step in outlining a
model for GAI identity development, the present paper explores
how (a) acculturation, (b) cultural values, and (c) conflicts in allegiances affect urban GAI identity development. Additionally, implications for mental health social service delivery will be dis-

cussed. Due to the lack of psychological studies on GAI identity, findings from the ethnic and gay and lesbian research will be used to illuminate the experience of urban GAIs. Prior to the discussion of the variables associated with GAI identity, a brief review of ethnic identity, gay and lesbian identity, and gay ethnic identity research will be highlighted.

IDENTITY RESEARCH

Many oppressed groups share common patterns in adjustment and resistance to oppression (Sue & Sue, 1990). There is evidence that a parallel process of racial and ethnic identity development exists for oppressed populations that involves moving from internalized negative attitudes about self and group to an actualized identity (Cross, 1978; Helms, 1990; Parham & Helms, 1985a, 1985b; Phinney, 1990; Walters, 1995). Although numerous frameworks and stages of minority identity development have been proposed by researchers to investigate identity processes, the racial and ethnic identity attitude studies have had the greatest empirical success in demonstrating the relationship between ethnic identity and mental health, self-esteem, and self-concept (Atkinson, Morten, & Sue, 1990; Helms, 1990; Phinney, 1990). Collapsing the different ethnic/racial identity stage models, a four-stage progression emerges that stands as the framework in which identity processes unfold (Cross; 1978; Morten, Atkinson, & Sue, 1983; Parham & Helms, 1985a, 1985b; Phinney, 1990; Sue, 1992; Walters, 1995). The first stage involves an underdeveloped racial/ethnic awareness and identification with the dominant culture's values and institutions. The second stage includes an experience that activates awareness of the significance of one's race and racial oppression. The third stage consists of an immersion experience into one's own culture and is characterized by anger towards dominant society and individuals. The fourth stage is characterized by integration of a positive self and group identity (Atkinson, Morten, & Sue, 1983; Cross, 1978; Parham & Helms, 1985a, 1985b; Phinney, 1990; Sue, 1992; Walters, 1995).

Walters (1995) expanded the ethnic and racial identity models of Cross (1978), Helms (1990), and Sue (1990) in creating the Urban American Indian Identity (UAII) model and scale (UAIIS). Like other racial identity models, the UAII model consists of four stages (i.e., internalization, marginalization, externalization, actualization) that tap into a process of identity development from internalized oppression and self/group deprecation to a positive, integrated self and group identity (Walters, 1995). According to the UAII model, identity is formed in the context of the person (self identity), the person's group (group identity), the person's social environment (urban environment), and the historical relationship with the dominant society (dominant group environment and institutional responses). Each stage contains the following five identity dimensions: political (e.g., Indian land and treaty rights); racial (e.g., phenotypical features, mixed-bloodedness); ethnic (e.g., sense of shared heritage); cultural (e.g., cultural values, knowledge, language); and spiritual (e.g., sacred sites) attitudes regarding one's Indian self and group identity (Walters, 1993, 1995). Initial results indicated that the UAIIS is reliable, and that the model predicts depression, self-esteem, and other psychological wellness indicators (Walters, 1995).

Research on gay and lesbian identity has consisted mainly of retrospective reports and has focused on the individual's coming out process. Cass's (1984) gay and lesbian identity model has received the most empirical attention. Her six-stage model describes the coming out process for gays and lesbians as consisting of "identity-confusion (Who am I?); comparison (I am different); tolerance (I am probably gay); acceptance (I am gay); pride (I am gay!); and synthesis (My gayness is one part of me)" (Walters & Simoni, 1993, p. 94). Walters and Simoni (1993) applied the Parham and Helms' (1985a, 1985b) racial identity model to gays and lesbians and observed a parallel process of group identity attitude development.

Psychological studies on gays and lesbians of color and their corresponding identity development have been conducted on small samples of Mexican Americans (Espin, 1987; Hidalgo & Hidalgo, 1976; Morales, 1989); African Americans (Hendin, 1969; Icard, 1986; Johnson, 1982; Loiacano, 1989; Mays, 1985); and Asian Americans (Chan, 1989; Warren, 1980; Wooden, Kawaksaki, & Mayeda, 1983). Researchers studying ethnic gay and lesbian identity combine the racial and ethnic identity attitude models (i.e., Atkinson, Morten, & Sue, 1983; Cross, 1978; Helms, 1990; Parham, 1989; Parham & Helms, 1985a, 1985b; Phinney, 1990; Sue, 1992) with the Cass (1984) gay and lesbian identity model.

Combining the ethnic identity models and the coming out model, Morales (1989) proposed a five-stage ethnic gay and lesbian identity model that consists of denial of conflicts (I am not clear on what my gayness means to me and my ethnicity is no big deal); bisexual versus gay/lesbian (I prefer to identify as bisexual, even if my behavior and relationships are primarily homosexual); conflicts in allegiances (I identify as gay and not ethnic around gays and ethnic and not gay around other ethnics); establishing priorities in allegiances (I am ethnic and resent the racism in the gay community or I am gay and resent the homophobia in my ethnic community); and integration (I am both ethnic and gay).

The ethnic gay and lesbian identity research describes two linear processes that occur simultaneously, one in terms of ethnic identity, and the other in terms of the acquisition of a gay and lesbian identity through the coming out process. The ethnic identity models focus on group identity and the corresponding attitudes that one has toward one's own group, whereas the "coming out" model focuses on the awareness of self identity and coming to terms with the realization of being gay. However, none of the models addresses ethnic gay or lesbian identity as it changes over time throughout adulthood (i.e., post "coming out" as gay or lesbian). Moreover, by combining ethnic identity models with a "coming out" model, the relationship between gay male and lesbian identity and the psychological attitudes ethnic gays and lesbians have toward being a member of the gay and lesbian community (i.e., group identity attitudes: Walters & Simoni, 1993) is left unexamined.

ACCULTURATION

Acculturation of ethnic minorities into the dominant European-American culture and its effects on ethnic gay and lesbian identity development have not been adequately addressed. One cannot discuss GAI identity development without understanding how decades of colonization and urbanization have repressed much of the historical Indian traditions that incorporated multiple gender roles and same-sex sexuality. Thus, acculturation (the indoctrination of White Western values among urban American Indians) and its impact on GAI identity development merit further theoretical attention.

Many researchers have noted that same sex relationships had a place, and in many instances a sacred, spiritual place, in several Indian societies (Blackwood, 1985; Williams, 1986). Although there is considerable controversy over the gender role, spiritual role, and the sexual role of the "Berdache" (an inappropriate French term used by many researchers because it means a young man or boy who is the passive recipient of anal intercourse), evidence suggests that same-sex unions were at the very least tolerated and in some instances celebrated (Callender & Kochems, 1986; Williams, 1986). Acculturative processes have altered such attitudes.

Recently, researchers have begun to discuss a multi-dimensional process whereby acculturation and ethnic identity consist of two independent processes that occur simultaneously. They are not separate ends of a bipolar continuum, but are separate dimensions that independently vary. Studies now support this multidimensional view (Der Karabetian, 1980; Hutnik, 1985; Kemnitzer, 1978; Mendoza, 1989). In the urban environment, acculturation tends to be accelerated, leading to more negative attitudes and values toward GAIs. One result is the increase in intolerance of same-sex relationships and the erosion of GAIs traditional status among many tribal nations. As a result, GAIs are deprived of learning valuable survival skills and are vulnerable to internalizing a negative identity as a GAI. However, GAIs who have had access to positive GAI role models or understanding of such roles within their own tribe are more resilient and less likely to have a negative gay Indian identity in the urban environment as well.

More traditional Indians tend to respect GAIs, while the more acculturated Indians tend to devalue and stigmatize them (Williams, 1986). Although there is considerable individual variability in level of internalization of negative dominant group attitudes toward GAIs, the general attitudes of support or rejection due to acculturation warrant discussion. Thus, more acculturated Indians (gay and non-gay) tend to internalize the dominant societies' negative attitudes toward GAIs and the less acculturated tend to rely on internalized tribal beliefs in shaping their attitudes toward GAIs.

Among more acculturated Indians, a general feeling toward GAIs is fear, which is not only directed toward GAIs but is generalized to anything that represents "the old ways" (Allen, 1986). Paula Gunn Allen (1986) notes that the increase in negative feelings is the result of colonization and acculturation by Euro-Americans. She writes:

> The process by which external conquest and colonization [has] become internalized among the colonized . . . has steadily grown among them as they have traded traditional tribal values for Christian industrial ones. . . . Other Indians, more acculturated and highly Christianized, treat the presence of . . . homosexuality among them with fear and loathing. They do not confine that loathing to homosexuality but direct it to other aspects of tribal ceremonial life. (pp. 198-199)

Indoctrination of negative attitudes toward GAIs among non-gay Indians and among GAIs has been primarily through the (in some cases forced) adoption of Western Christian religions. The more acculturated generally have adopted Western Christian philosophies which are antithetical to positive attitudes toward homosexuality. Thus, Euro-American spirituality has had a significant impact on the internalization of negative attitudes toward GAIs among Indian peoples. In turn, the negative attitudes that non-gay Indians express verbally or nonverbally have an impact on GAI identity development. Psychologists note that the impact on GAIs is ". . . that lesbians and gay men of color and those from ethnic or religious backgrounds with especially negative attitudes about homosexuality would find it difficult to come out and to develop a positive gay male or lesbian identity" (Garnets & Kimmel, 1991, p. 160).

The denial of the existence of GAIs among some more acculturated Indians contributes to the invisibility of positive cultural referents for same-sex relationships and affects GAI identity. Denial of existence of gays and lesbians as being a part of the ethnic community has also been documented among Asians and Blacks (Chan, 1989; Loiacano, 1989). This denial forces GAIs to choose between being Indian and gay as if the two were incompatible. Thus, GAIs are pressured to deny important aspects of themselves and their lives to gain Indian community support. Ben the Dancer (1988) points out that "this is very hard on the gay [Indian] individual, because of the strong home and community pressures to conform and strong feelings of belonging to a tribe" (p. 132).

Many scholars and historians have noted that in recent years there has been an active return to identifying traditional, tribal-specific understandings of same-sex relationships among GAIs and non-gay American Indians. Not coincidentally this movement has followed the rise in overall tribal nationalism and the Red Power movement of the 1970s. As a result of the return to more traditional practices and elders, there has been an increase in positive attitudes toward GAIs among more traditional Indians. Ben the Dancer (1988) notes the following:

> Indian gays on the reservation are subjected to the same con-servative morality as Indian gays off the reservation in Ameri-can society. This creates intolerance and segregates Indians even more . . . luckily, there are Indians fighting to keep Indian traditions and values strong. There are also gay Indians who blend their gay lifestyle with tradition and who have made a good place in American society for themselves and others. (p. 132-133)

Williams (1986) states that a protective circle exists around GAIs in some traditional communities. Scholars have noted that many traditional Indians prefer not to discuss the subject with non-In-dians, not out of homophobia, but for cultural survival reasons (Allen, 1986; Williams, 1986). For example, traditionalists' silence on the issue to non-Indians reflects a protective stance where they are unwilling to subject their respected traditions to ridicule and potential appropriation among non-Indians. Additionally, by main-taining silence they are ensuring continuity and survival of their values and tribal ways. However, much of this support has been primarily documented in reservation or rural Indian communities and remains inadequate in urban Indian communities (Williams, 1986). Thus, many urban GAIs do not have the luxury of having a traditional frame of reference or protective circle of traditional el-ders.

CULTURAL VALUES

Researchers studying ethnic gay and lesbian identity have noted that cultural values are critical variables shaping self-concept, the coming out process, coping skills, and psychological well-being (Berry, Kim, Minde, & Mok, 1987; Chan, 1989; Cornell, 1988; Hendin, 1969; Johnson, 1982; Kraus & Buffler, 1979; Loiacano, 1989; Mays, 1985; Morales, 1989; Trembel, Schneider, & Appathurai, 1989; Warren, 1980; Wooden et al., 1983). Additionally, some cultural values contribute to the hesitancy of ethnic gays and lesbians to come out in their ethnic communities as well as contribute to fear of rejection and stigmatization within their communities (Chan, 1989; Hendin, 1969; Johnson, 1982; Loiacano, 1989; Mays, 1985; Morales, 1989; Trembel, Schneider, & Appathurai, 1989; Warren, 1980; Wooden, Kawaksaki, & Mayeda, 1983).

The difficulty in GAIs' acknowledging their sexual orientation to other family or community members is in part due to the conflict between gay and lesbian cultural values (which generally reflect European-American values) and Indian cultural values (Garnets & Kimmel, 1991). Cultural values play a significant role in creating and defining parameters as to expected cultural roles and norms. Specific cultural values define appropriate social and cultural roles for Indian people. One example of a cultural value among Indians is a strong emphasis on family and kin networks. Among other ethnic groups such as Blacks and Latinos, propagation of the race and fulfilling the role of "parent" are seen as integral to being Black or Latino. Thus, any deviations from such roles are construed as a betrayal of one's appropriate roles and identity. Hence, conflicts between gay and lesbian cultural values and American Indian cultural values also contribute to GAIs' lack of openness and visibility in their Indian communities and families (Chan, 1989).

Among American Indians, several other Indian cultural values are in direct conflict with values held by the gay and lesbian community. The value of "coming out" and being openly gay is valued as part of healthy psychosocial development among the gay and lesbian community (Cass, 1984). However, cooperation, a second Indian cultural value, emphasizes ". . . security in being a member of the group and in not being singled out and placed in a position above or below others" (California Department of Education, 1991). The Indian value of cooperation is opposed to the gay and lesbian value of being individualistic and placing one's needs above the group and to self-identify as different and "out."

A third related value held by Indian peoples is to strive for anonymity where ". . . the needs of the group are considered over those of the individual" (California Department of Education, 1991). This value also is in stark contrast to the value of coming out. Coming out requires one to openly identify oneself and draw attention to oneself, a process that is considered disrespectful within the Indian community.

Indian cultural values also are used in defining how non-gay Indians react to GAIs. For example, GAIs' deviation from their cultural role is dealt with through teasing or criticism by other Indian community members as can be seen by the following example:

> A lot of them did criticize me. They'd say "Well, you're out there, you're trying to be different. You're trying to say yes, you're an Indian, but you're trying to be a different Indian than the rest of us." So it took time for us to educate them and tell them. (Pahe, 1988, p. 111)

One way Indians show disapproval of GAIs is silence and placidity. Indian people generally believe that people are not to be controlled, but a socially appropriate way to express disapproval and, in effect, provide a form of social control is through silence. This is not to say that silence always means disapproval, for silence can also mean, among other things, respect. However, the following example illustrates how silence may be used to tacitly acknowledge some form of disapproval:

> It's not anything that's ever talked about. It's not dealt with. You're a member of the family, that's the priority. The chain of command in our family is real sturdy in that the oldest boy is more or less the father. So we all work real hard to make sure we don't do anything or say anything that is going to upset him. (Pahe, 1988, p. 107)

Conflicts in value systems create tension in resolving the demands of both communities within GAI individuals. Such conflicts and tensions among GAIs increase feelings of estrangement in both communities. GAIs attempt to cope with this estrangement in many ways. One way that many GAIs cope with such tensions is by splitting off the gay aspect of themselves in the Indian community and remaining silent with respect to that part of themselves. An illustration of this coping strategy can be seen in the following example:

> There are gay men who live on the reservation, and they lead happy lives. Your sexual life is your own business. If you take an active part in the life of the reservation, if you give input and show you care, you will be accepted. What matters is being a Hupa Indian. (Prather, 1988, p. 125)

Thus, as long as Indian identity remains the primary reference group orientation within the GAI individual, there is less stigmatization from the Indian community. Although in this example, it could be argued that the GAI individual above has integrated his gayness as an aspect of his life and is not downplaying it because of a lack of internal integration. However, for many GAIs who are still attempting to integrate their identities, denying and downplaying the gay or lesbian aspect of their identity may reflect a lack of integration and can be particularly painful. Coping by splitting creates the illusion that one has to choose one identity over the other or to the exclusion of the other part of one's identity.

Likewise, in the gay community, GAIs may downplay their Indianness. Of course, this may be in part to protect and preserve that aspect of themselves from discrimination within the gay and lesbian community. The splitting nevertheless affects identity integration, social stress, and psychological well-being (Herdt, 1989).

In sum, there are several cultural conflicts with which GAIs have to come to terms. First, the varying levels of negative aspects of acculturation among urban Indians suggest that there may be more homophobia in this community (as opposed to rural Indian communities) and less access to positive gay or lesbian Indian traditional roles. Second, gay and lesbian community values often are at odds with Indian community values. Third, both communities demand that the gay/lesbian Indian individual stay true to the cultural values of that community thereby creating pressures to choose one community over the other as a primary means of self-identification. Furthermore, the difficulties in integrating Indian cultural values with gay and lesbian community values depend on the level of acculturation of the gay or lesbian Indian individual. Finally, this dichotomy creates a split within the individual and makes it difficult for him or her to integrate a positive identity as a gay American Indian. Acculturation and cultural values affect GAI identity development and the attitudes found in urban Indian communities. At the root of this problem in splitting is the artificial creation of conflicts in allegiances that are the result of two communities dealing with their own oppressed group statuses.

CONFLICTS IN ALLEGIANCES

Conflicts in allegiances are another critical aspect of GAI identity development. A critical task that ethnic gays and lesbians face in identity development is to integrate conflicting allegiances that arise as the result of being a member of two oppressed groups (Chan, 1989; Hendin, 1969; Johnson, 1982; Loiacano, 1989; Mays, 1985; Morales, 1989; Warren, 1980; Wooden et al., 1983). Research indicates that having a double minority group status creates conflicts in allegiances between the gay and lesbian community and the ethnic community (Garnets & Kimmel, 1991; Loiacano, 1989; Mays, 1985; Morales, 1989). GAIs participate in disparate social worlds which include their gay and lesbian community, their Indian community and the dominant culture. Walking in multiple worlds requires a delicate balancing act that demands crossing many boundaries and multiple social roles. Thus, Indian gays and lesbians have a double or triple (e.g., American Indian, lesbian, woman) minority status and experience discrimination within their own culture (as a gay person); within the gay and lesbian community (as an ethnic minority); and within the dominant group (as both an ethnic person and as a gay or lesbian person; Garnets & Kimmel, 1991; Morales, 1989). As Morales (1989) points out, "it requires constant effort to maintain oneself in three different social worlds, each of which fails to support significant aspects of a person's life" (p. 217). Consequently, for GAIs, a double minority group status creates multiple challenges in negotiating these statuses and forging a positive identity.

Conflicts in allegiances arise due to the discrimination that exists both within the Indian community (homophobia) and the gay and lesbian community (racism). Historically, the lesbian and gay community has exhibited racial discrimination toward gays and lesbians of color. Discrimination has taken many forms. Asian-Americans, for example, report that they feel stereotyped as "erotic" or are unacknowledged in the gay and lesbian community (Chan, 1989).

Likewise, many GAIs have had to deal with being romanticized, eroticized, and unacknowledged. Jaimes and Halsey (1992) write:

> Another increasingly volatile issue . . . has been the appropriation and distortion of indigenous traditions concerning homosexuality by both "radical" or lesbian feminists and gay male activists. Particularly offensive have been non-Indian efforts to convert the indigenous custom of treating homosexuals . . . as persons endowed with special spiritual powers into a polemic for mass organization within the dominant society. (p. 333)

Like other groups, Indians may be viewed as "inferior" in the gay community and are subjected to discrimination in admittance to gay bars, non-acknowledgement, and sexual stereotyping (DeMarco, 1983; Morales, 1989).

In addition to being discriminated against by the gay and lesbian community, many GAIs similarly experience rejection, stigmatization, and homophobia within their own Indian community. Non-gay Indians may see identification with another oppressed group as being an unnecessary burden on an already oppressed status with which the GAI individual has to deal. Another difficulty is that heterosexual Indians may experience identification as gay or lesbian by the GAI individual as an abandonment of priorities in fighting racial or cultural oppression.

There tends to be a conflict between a fear of being stigmatized by the ethnic community versus the loss of support in the lesbian or gay community for being ethnic (Chan, 1989; Espin, 1987). In a study of 13 Japanese gay men, Wooden et al. found that the respondents were fearful of being visibly active in the gay community due to being potentially rejected by the Japanese community. Likewise, in Indian communities, the fear of rejection contributes to GAIs feeling like outsiders within the Indian community, isolated from their families and kin networks (Espin, 1987; Garnets & Kimmel, 1991; Loiacano, 1989).

The effects of how much one of the communities (Indian vs. gay) is perceived to be discriminatory varies by gender (Chan, 1989; Espin, 1987; Garnets & Kimmel, 1990; Mays, 1985). Studies of gender differences among gay men and lesbians of color have shown that ethnic gay men generally experience discrimination based on homosexuality first and race second. On the other hand, lesbians of color reportedly experience race or gender based discrimination first, and sexual orientation second (Chan, 1989; Espin, 1987; Mays, 1985). Moreover, women of color perceive greater discrimination because of their triple minority status as Indian, woman, and lesbian (Chan, 1989). As a result of GAIs being compartmentalized regarding the sexual and ethnic aspects of themselves, many feel as if they do not completely belong to one group or the other, thereby creating difficulty in consolidating an identity as both an Indian and as a gay or lesbian individual.

In terms of the impact that conflicts in allegiances have on identity development, there have been contradictory reports concerning which group the individual feels most comfortable with and which group they most strongly identify with. Research on gays and lesbians reflects mixed feelings. Espin (1987) noted that Latina lesbians more strongly identified with a White lesbian community, whereas among Asian lesbians Chan (1989) noted that there was a mix in terms of who one identifies with depending on the needs of the individual and the situation. In terms of GAIs, the strength of identification probably depends on the situational context and the level of acculturation. Furthermore, the comfort level is dependent upon the acculturation level of the Indian community or family/kin network with which the GAI associates. Hence, if the Indian kin network is accepting of GAIs, then the GAI may identify more strongly with the Indian community. However, if the Indian community is not accepting, then there may be greater conflict in integrating a GAI identity within it.

Many researchers report that gays and lesbians of color prefer to have both parts of themselves acknowledged by both their ethnic community and the gay and lesbian community. However, many GAIs and other ethnic gays and lesbians report difficulty in achieving this integration (Chan, 1989; Espin, 1987; Garnets & Kimmel, 1991). According to Morales (1989), "a common feeling engendered by the complexity in lifestyle is one of being unable to integrate the pieces of one's life . . . complications that arise may inhibit one's ability to adapt and to maximize personal potentials" (p. 219). Such pressures lead to heightened feelings of anxiety, tension, isolation, depression, anger, and problems in integrating aspects of the self (Morales, 1989). The loss of social support for all salient aspects of one's self compromises one's access to much needed social support, coping assistance, and survival skills.

TOWARDS A MODEL OF GAI IDENTITY DEVELOPMENT

Jones (1991) has called for research that explores the role of identity development and the attitudes toward the self and one's ethnic group. Utilization of a developmental stage model is suggested for a GAI identity model because this framework has been empirically researched for other ethnic and cultural groups. Furthermore, developmental studies have had the most success in demonstrating the relationship between ethnic identity and self-identity attitudes, group identity attitudes, self-esteem, and self-concept (Helms, 1985; Parham, 1989; Parham & Helms, 1985a, 1985b; Phinney, 1990; Walters & Simoni, 1993). In addition, studies indicate that the developmental model accounts for multilevel processes (Parham & Helms, 1985). For example, identity attitude researchers utilizing the developmental framework view identity as the product of the interaction between the social environment and the psychological self (Kitano, 1991). The trend in identity research suggests that a multilevel approach should explore both between (gay and Indian) and within group (Indian) interactions (Jones, 1991; Rogoff & Morelli, 1989; Sue, 1992). Urban GAI identity development must be understood within this multilevel context.

Urban GAI identity attitudes are formed within the context of the sociohistorical interaction between the dominant society and Indian people. Urban GAI identity consists of both self-identity and group identity. Self-identity includes the attitudes that one has about one's attributes, capacities, and behaviors (Sue, 1992) as an Indian and as a gay person. Group identity consists of the attitudes that a GAI individual has regarding Indian people as a group and gay and lesbian people as a group (e.g., their group attributes, capacities, and behaviors). Hence, self and group identity attitudes together form GAI Indian identity.

From the literature on identity models, we can draw eight parallels to GAI identity development. First, GAIs may be highly ethnically identified and highly gay identified simultaneously, although the two are not necessarily correlated. As Oetting and Beauvais (1990-1991), in their Orthogonal Cultural Identification Theory, point out, cultural identification is an orthogonal process where identification with one culture does not necessarily mean a lesser identification with another culture. Thus, cultural identification consists of independent identities where individuals can have a unicultural, bicultural, or multicultural identification simultaneously. Second, GAI group identity attitudes may be high or low on either continuum. For example, one could have positive attitudes toward Indians as a group and toward the self as Indian (e.g., Walters, 1995) but hold negative attitudes toward gays as a group and toward oneself as a GAI (e.g., Walters & Simoni, 1993). Third, the level of development in terms of coming out to oneself and to the community affects gay and lesbian self- and group identity and, therefore, needs to be considered as an added dimension to a GAI identity model.

Fourth, urban GAIs may pass through different stages throughout their lifetime (stage models are not necessarily linear [Grotevant, 1987; Parham, 1989]). Urban GAIs may "spiral" back through earlier stages at higher levels, experiencing early stage traits if resistance becomes low and if external impingements increase feelings of isolation, anomie, and powerlessness (Walters & Simoni, 1993). Furthermore, urban Indian people may possess qualities of the different stages simultaneously.

Fifth, a model of GAI identity attitude development needs to consider the acculturation level of both the GAI individual and the Indian community and family to which he or she belongs. Tribal specific histories need to be taken into account because some tribes are more acculturated than other tribes. The urban GAI individual may not have had access to a reservation, language, traditional spiritual practices, or other GAI role models. Acculturation and the variations in starting points and attitudes in this stage process may reflect at what generation the individual arrived in the urban environment. Hence, third and fourth generation urban Indians are more likely to be more acculturated than those who recently moved to the city. Moreover, second or third generation Indians may be more homophobic, having been exposed to more negative dominant group attitudes toward homosexuality; whereas fourth generation urban Indians, although more acculturated, have been exposed to more positive attitudes by the dominant culture toward homosexuality, and therefore reflect more positive attitudes toward GAIs. Thus, level of acculturation (including the generation level) is the fifth dimension that needs to be incorporated into an urban GAI identity model.

Sixth and seventh, the model needs to address the cultural values that are still held intact by GAI individuals and their kin networks as well as account for how conflicts in allegiances are contributing to the difficulties in consolidating an integrated GAI identity. Eighth, the model should be inclusive of the dual dimensionality of the two group identity attitude development processes (Indian identity and gay and lesbian group identity) in conjunction with self-identity development (i.e., stage of coming out). Hence, the GAI individual could have positive attitudes toward being Indian (e.g., Stage 4–Actualization: Walters, 1995), and toward being a member of the gay community (e.g., Stage 4–Internalization: Walters & Simoni, 1993). The GAI individual may also have accepted his or her gayness as an integral part of self (Stage 6–Identity Acceptance: Cass, 1984).

IMPLICATIONS FOR MENTAL HEALTH SERVICE DELIVERY

Too often identity researchers have emphasized a deficit model focusing on the negatives in identity development among oppressed groups. To counter this, social service professionals, and in particular, clinicians, need to focus on GAI clients' resilience and positive coping. This will help to counter the negative aspects of dealing with a disparaged status in a society that oppresses both Indian peoples and gays and lesbians. Additionally, by focusing on the GAI clients' strengths, the clinician, in effect, reminds the GAI client of his or her sources of strength and reinforces a positive self-image.

A second recommendation for effective and culturally sensitive clinical intervention is that the GAI clients' level of acculturation and the corresponding cultural values and conflict in allegiances be assessed. These three factors help the clinician identify areas in need of intervention. For example, if the GAI client is having difficulty in coping with conflicts in allegiances, finding ways in which the client can begin to integrate the disparate worlds may be helpful (e.g., accessing GAI organizations, support groups). Additionally, if the client is not highly acculturated, identifying traditional ways in which GAIs had a role that is specific to his or her tribe may also be helpful. In exploring acculturation, it is important to note if incorporating other members of the clients' family, tribe, elders, or medicine persons may be necessary to help the client integrate a positive identity.

Another intervention includes helping the client to find culturally relevant ways to "come out" that do not deny or split off the gay or lesbian or Indian aspect of self. If the problems of the GAI client are less internal (i.e., the client is coping fairly well) and are more external (i.e., due to homophobia or racism), then identifying ways to educate others or to become active in fighting such oppression can be explored as well. Thus, acculturation level, cultural values, and conflicts in allegiances provide information as to the appropriate areas of intervention, whether it is within the individual in terms of helping the GAI client to integrate both identities or whether it is external (i.e., fighting homophobia or racism).

Debunking stereotypes and providing access to positive GAI role models that are tribal specific to the GAI client's Indian culture are also important interventions. Dependent upon the level of integration of a GAI identity, these interventions may be more fruitful in earlier GAI identity development. Additionally, involvement in more gay and/or Indian contacts may be an appropriate intervention if one or the other is neglected due to the conflicts in allegiances.

In exploring gay and lesbian and Indian group identity attitudes, clinicians should be aware of the interplay between intrapsychic problems and external, systemic factors such as homophobia and racism (Walters & Simoni, 1993). Mental health social service providers' effectiveness will be due in part to their ability to differentiate among these factors (Trimble, 1981; Trimble & LaFromboise, 1985). Thus, both Indian and non-Indian, gay or non-gay clinicians need to educate themselves to understand the complexities of GAI identity development. Understanding the multidimensionality of the GAI experience and the corresponding factors that contribute to identity development, helps clinicians and social service administrators to develop more culturally sensitive treatment strategies and agency programs. For example, the level of group and self-identity attitudes of GAIs may help administrators and clinicians identify preference for a gay clinician, a non-gay Indian clinician or gay Indian clinician (depending on the levels of GAI identity attitudes) as has been demonstrated with other ethnic groups.

In terms of social service delivery on a macro level, a GAI identity model may help increase GAI mental health service utilization and client retention in agency programs. Thus, identifying issues that are pertinent to GAI identity development can assist social service administrators and clinicians in developing culturally relevant assessment strategies, treatment plans, and intra-agency coordination. Moreover, it can provide a multidimensional understanding of how dual minority group status affects mental health functioning. Additionally, positive aspects of coping and resilience among GAIs can be identified as well to facilitate prevention and intervention efforts by social service providers.

In terms of research, a GAI model of identity development warrants further attention and can contribute to a growing body of knowledge on identity development in general. In particular, future research needs to examine sex and tribal differences among GAIs to determine within group variabilities. This will help to facilitate greater understanding of the role of triple (homophobia, racism, and sexism) group oppression in the development of GAI identity. Additionally, the differences between rural, reservation, and urban GAI identity development need to be delineated. Understanding such complexities will help mental health social service providers distinguish among tricultural and intertribal issues and variations (Walters & Simoni, 1993). Furthermore, applied research will help to delineate how GAI identity development affects self-concept, other mental health problems, and mental health service utilization.

LaFromboise (1988) and Moncher, Holden and Trimble (1990) advocate development of a "bicultural competence repertoire" to assist Indian peoples in developing adaptive coping responses to the interaction between their tribal culture and that of the majority culture. LaFromboise (1982) states that bicultural competence helps Indians to ". . . blend the adaptive values and roles of both the culture in which they were raised and the culture by which they are surrounded" (p. 12). Perhaps it is time to expand the bicultural competence schema to include the within group diversity of American Indian communities, and to include gay and lesbian American Indians in our research and direct practice efforts. In embracing Indian diversity, we as social service providers glimpse the multidimensionality of identity and are given an opportunity to enrich our social service delivery system. More importantly, in a society that oppresses, we can create a safe space for urban GAIs to explore their identity issues and confront the daily challenges to GAI continuity and survival.

REFERENCES

Allen, P. G. (1986). *The sacred hoop.* Boston: Beacon Press.

Atkinson, D., Morten, G., & Sue, D. (1983). *Counseling American minorities.* Dubuque, IA: W. C. Brown.

Ben the Dancer (1988). Gay American Indians. In W. Roscoe (Ed.), *Living the spirit: A gay American Indian anthology* (pp. 131-133). NY: St. Martins Press.

Berlin, I. N. (1987). Aspects of changing native American cultures on child development. *Journal of Community Psychology, 15,* 299-306.

Berry, J., Kim, U., Minde, T., & Mok, D. (1987). Comparative studies of acculturative stress. *International Migration Review, 21,* 491-511.

Blackwood, E. (1985). Sexuality and gender in certain Native American tribes: The case of cross-gender females. *Signs, 10,* 27-42.

California Department of Education. (1991). *Indian values, attitudes and behaviors, together with educational considerations,* pp. 25-32. Sacramento, CA: Bill Honig, State Superintendent of Public Instruction.

Callender, C., & Kochems, L. (1986). Men and not-men: Male gender-mixing statuses and homosexuality. *Journal of Homosexuality, 11,* 165-178.

Cass, V. C. (1984). Homosexual identity formation: Testing a theoretical model. *Journal of Sex Research, 20,* 143-167.

Chan, C. S. (1989). Issues of identity development among Asian American lesbians and gay men. *Journal of Counseling and Development, 68,* 16-20.

Cornell, S. (1988). The transformations of tribes: Organization and self-concept in Native American ethnicities. *Ethnic and Racial Studies, 11,* 27-47.

Cross, W. (1978). The Thomas and Cross models of psychological nigrescence: A literature review. *Journal of Black Psychology, 4,* 13-31.

DeMarco, J. (1983). Gay racism. In M. J. Smith (Ed.), *Black men/White men: A gay anthology* (pp. 109-118). San Francisco: Gay Sunshine Press.

Der Karabetian, A. (1980). Relation of two cultural identities of Armenian-Americans. *Psychological Reports, 47,* 123-148.

Espin, O. M. (1987). Issues of identity in the psychology of Latina lesbians: In the Boston Lesbian Psychologies Collective (Eds.), *Lesbian psychologies: Explorations and challenges* (pp. 35-51). Urbana-Champaign, IL: University of Illinois Press.

Garnets, L., & Kimmel, D. (1991). Lesbian and gay male dimensions in the psychological study of human diversity. In J. D. Goodchilds (Ed.), *Psychological perspectives on human diversity: Masters lecturers* (pp. 143-189). Washington, DC: American Psychological Association.

Grotevant, H. (1987). Toward a model of identity formation. *Journal of Adolescent Research, 2,* 203-222.

Helms, J. (1985). Toward a theoretical explanation of the effects of race on counseling: A black and white model. *The Counseling Psychologist, 12,* 153-165.

Helms, J. (1990). *Black and White racial identity attitudes: Theory, practice, and research.* NY: Greenwood Press.

Hendin, H. (1969). *Black suicide.* NY: Basic Books.

Herdt, G. (1989). Introduction: Gay and lesbian youth, emergent identities, and cultural scenes at home and abroad. In G. Herdt (Ed.), *Gay and lesbian youth* (pp. 4-33). NY: Harrington Park Press.

Hidalgo, A., & Hidalgo, C. (1976). The Puerto Rican lesbian and the Puerto Rican community. *Journal of Homosexuality, 2,* 109-121.

Hutnik, N. (1985). Aspects of identity in a multi-ethnic society. *New Community, 12,* 298-309.

Icard, L. (1986). Black gay men and conflicting social identities: Sexual orientation versus racial identity. In J. Gripton & M. Valentich (Eds.), Special issue of the *Journal of Social Work and Human Sexuality: Social work practice in sexual problems, 4* (1/2), 83-93.

Jaimes, M. A., & Halsey, T. (1992). American Indian women: At the center of indigenous resistance in North America. In M. A. Jaimes (Ed.), *The state of Native America: Genocide, colonization, and resistance* (pp. 311-344). Boston, MA: South End Press.

Jarvenpa, R. (1985). The political economy and political ethnicity of American Indian adaptations and identities. *Ethnic and Racial Studies, 8,* 29-48.

Johnson, J. (1982*). The influence of assimilation on the psychosocial adjustment of Black homosexual men.* Unpublished dissertation, California School of Professional Psychology, Berkeley, CA.

Jones, J. J. (1991). Psychological models of race: What have they been and what should they be? In J. D. Goodchilds (Ed.), *Psychological perspectives on human diversity in America: Lecture series* (pp. 3-46). Washington, DC: American Psychological Association.

Kemnitzer, L. S. (1978). Adjustment and value conflict in urbanizing Dakota Indians measured by Q-Sort technique. *American Anthropologist, 75,* 687-707.

Kim, J. (1981). *The process of Asian-American identity development: A study of Japanese women's perceptions of their struggle to achieve positive identities.* Unpublished doctoral dissertation, University of Massachusetts, Massachusetts.

Kitano, H. (1991). *Race relations* (4th ed.). Englewood Cliffs: NJ: Prentice-Hall.

Kraus, R. F., & Buffler, P. A. (1979). Sociocultural stress and the American Native in Alaska: An analysis of changing patterns of psychiatric illness and alcohol abuse among Alaska Natives. *Culture, Medicine and Psychiatry, 3,* 111-151.

LaFromboise, T. D. (1988). American Indian mental health policy. *American Psychologist, 43,* 388-397.

Loiacano, D. K. (1989). Gay identity issues among Black Americans: Racism, homophobia, and the need for validation. *Journal of Counseling and Development, 68,* 21-25.

Mays, V. M. (1985). Black women working together: Diversity in same sex relationships. *Women's Studies International Forum, 8,* 67-71.

Mendoza, R. H. (1989). An empirical scale to measure type and degree of acculturation in Mexican-American adolescents and adults. *Journal of Cross-Cultural Psychology, 20,* 372-385.

Moncher, M., Holden, G. W., & Trimble, J. E. (1990). Substance abuse among Native American youth. *Journal of Consulting and Clinical Psychology, 58,* 408-415.

Morales, E. S. (1989). Ethnic minority families and minority gays and lesbians. *Marriage and Family Review, 14,* 217-239.

Oetting, E. R., & Beauvais, F. (1990-1991). Orthogonal cultural identification theory: The cultural identification of minority adolescents. *The International Journal of the Addictions, 25* (5A & 6A), 655-685.

Pahe, E. (1988). Speaking up. In W. Roscoe (Ed.), *Living the spirit: A Gay American Indian anthology* (pp. 104-116). NY: St. Martin's Press.

Parham, T. (1989). Cycles of psychological nigrescence. *The Counseling Psychologist, 17,* 187-226.

Parham, T., & Helms, J. (1985a). Attitudes of racial identity and self-esteem of Black students: An exploratory investigation. *Journal of College Student Personnel, 26* (2), 143-147.

Parham, T., & Helms, J. (1985b). Relation of racial identity attitudes to self-actualization and affective states of Black students. *Journal of Counseling Psychology, 32,* 431-440.

Phinney, J. (1990). Ethnic identity in adolescents and adults: Review of Research. *Psychological Bulletin, 108* (3), 499-514.

Prather, K. (1988). Becoming Indian. In W. Roscoe (Ed.), *Living the spirit: A Gay American Indian anthology* (pp. 119-127). NY: St. Martin's Press.

Rogoff, B., & Morelli, G. (1989). Clinical treatment of the nondisclosing Black client: A therapeutic paradox. *American Psychologist, 44,* 434-348.

Stiffarm, L. A., & Lane, P. (1992). The demography of native North Americans: A question of American Indian survival. In M. A. Jaimes (Ed.), *The state of Native America: Genocide, colonization, and resistance* (pp. 23-55). Boston MA: South End.

Sue, D. W., & Sue, D. (1990). *Counseling the culturally different: Theory and practice* (2nd. ed.). NY: John Wiley and Sons, Inc.

Sue, S. (1992). Ethnicity and culture in psychological research and practice. In J. D. Goodchilds (Ed.), *Psychological perspectives on human diversity in America: Masters lecture series* (pp. 51-85). Washington, DC: American Psychological Association.

Trembel, B., Schneider, M., & Appathurai, C. (1989). Growing up gay or lesbian in a multicultural context. *Journal of Homosexuality, 17* (3-4), 253-267.

Trimble, J. E. (1981). Value differentials and their importance in counseling American Indians. In P. B. Pederson, J. G. Draguns, W. J. Lonner, & J. E. Trimble (Eds.), *Counseling across cultures.* Honolulu, HI: University of Hawaii Press.

Trimble, J. E. (1987). Self-perception and perceived alienation among American Indians. *Journal of Community Psychology, 15* (3), 357-361.

Trimble, J. E., & LaFromboise, T. (1985). American Indians and the counseling process: Culture adaptation, and style. In P. B. Pederson (Ed.), *Handbook of cross-cultural counseling and therapy* (pp. 127-134). Westport, CT: Greenwood Press.

U.S. Bureau of the Census. (1994). *Census 1990.* Washington, DC: U.S. Government Printing Office.

Walters, K. L. (1993). *Urban American Indian identity development: A theoretical model.* Unpublished manuscript.

Walters, K. L., & Simoni, J. M. (1993). Lesbian and gay male group identity attitudes and self-esteem: Implications for counseling. *The Journal of Counseling Psychology, 40,* 94-99.

Walters, K. L. (1995*). Urban American Indian identity and psychological wellness.* Unpublished doctoral dissertation, University of California, Los Angeles.

Warren, C. (1980). Homosexuality and stigma. In J. Marmor (Ed.), *Homosexual behavior: A modern reappraisal* (pp. 123-141). NY: Basic Books.

Williams, W. L. (1986). *The spirit and the flesh: Sexual diversity in American Indian culture.* Boston: Beacon Press.

Wooden, W. S., Kawaksaki, H., & Mayeda, R. (1983). Lifestyles and identity maintenance among gay Japanese-American males. *Alternative Lifestyles, 5,* 236-243.

That's What They Say:
The Implications of American Indian
Gay and Lesbian Literature
for Social Service Workers

Judy A. Wright
Melodie A. Lopez
Lora L. Zumwalt

SUMMARY. This article presents an unusual approach to investigating lifestyle issues unique to the Native American gay and lesbian community. A review of poetry and literature composed by American Indian authors, both hetero- and homosexual, is presented to familiarize the reader with a number of issues important to human service providers. The blend of social and personal experiences presented in these works provides non-Indians with an insider's view of the Indian perspective on topics such as alcoholism, homelessness, and cultural discontinuity. *[Article copies available for a fee from The Haworth Document Delivery Service: 1-800-342-9678. E-mail address: getinfo@haworth.com]*

Judy A. Wright, MA, is a Master's of Social Work student, Department of Social Work, California State University, Long Beach. Melodie A. Lopez, BS, is a Master's of Social Work student, School of Social Work, University of California, Berkeley. Lora L. Zumwalt, BS, is a Master's of Social Work student, Department of Social Work, California State University, Long Beach.

[Haworth co-indexing entry note]: "That's What They Say: The Implications of American Indian Gay and Lesbian Literature for Social Service Workers." Wright, Judy A., Melodie A. Lopez, and Lora L. Zumwalt. Co-published simultaneously in *Journal of Gay & Lesbian Social Services* (The Haworth Press, Inc.) Vol. 6, No. 2, 1997, pp. 67-84; and: *Two Spirit People: American Indian Lesbian Women and Gay Men* (ed: Lester B. Brown) The Haworth Press, Inc., 1997, pp. 67-84; and: *Two Spirit People: American Indian Lesbian Women and Gay Men* (ed: Lester B. Brown) Harrington Park Press, an imprint of The Haworth Press, Inc., 1997, pp. 67-84. Single or multiple copies of this article are available for a fee from The Haworth Document Delivery Service [1-800-342-9678, 9:00 a.m. - 5:00 p.m. (EST). E-mail address: getinfo@haworth.com].

67

INTRODUCTION

Before beginning the discussion of Gay and Lesbian American Indian literature and social service issues, it is important, first, to take a look at several common misconceptions about American Indians in general, and, more specifically, those Indians who are Lesbians and Gays. While reading this article one must keep in mind that the term "American Indian" or "Native American" is misleading. We are not one homogeneous group. Each tribe has a distinct language, religion, culture, as well as tribal and community traditions. In the United States there are approximately 660 federally recognized tribes–360 located in the forty-eight states and another 300 in Alaska. These numbers do not include the hundreds of other groups which are still struggling with legal and governmental agencies to gain federal recognition. Therefore, one can immediately recognize that, when discussing any topic pertaining to American Indians, reductionist thought and stereotypes serve only to shroud the truths. In an attempt to avoid further generalizations and convey the tribal diversity of the poets and writers cited in this paper, their tribal affiliation has been parenthetically inserted after their names.

A second issue of importance is the definition of the Lesbian or Gay American Indian. A number of modern American Indian groups maintain belief in and practice of ancient traditional belief systems that do not apply social definitions of gender identity in terms of the Cartesian dualism common to industrialized Western cultures. Other Indian groups do. In fact, there is currently a debate among several tribal groups in the United States that centers on the validity of describing gays and lesbians as truly "other-gendered" persons. Each clan has its own specific worldview of alternate genders and they range from the social, spiritual and personal acceptance of a third, and even fourth gender, to outright denial of any concept beyond the Western gender-dyad (Grahn, 1984; Greenberg, 1986; Jacobs & Cromwell, 1992; Roscoe, 1987).

The Gay American Indian (GAI) History Project of 1984 found over 200 tribes as having specific titles for other gendered tribal members (Roscoe, 1987). Furthermore, these identifications did not imply the same physically orientated concept of gender as does the word "homosexual." For example, in conducting interviews, one of our contacts explained that the English translated phrase for gays among his people in Northern California is "treats him/her like a wife." As demonstrated by this instance, many of the various Indian terms used to refer to gender identifications tend to be descriptive rather than taxonomic. In addition, many of the Indian descriptors, which have become popularized in recent publications, have also become bastardized in the process of "popularization," and have lost their original meaning. So as not to add to the confusion, we have opted to use the common terms gay and lesbian.

Locating literature by or about lesbian and gay American Indians is fairly difficult. Many early anthropological works reflect Eurocentric biases common to the era in which they were created, generally the late-nineteenth century. As such, the anthropologist either ignored sexual identity as a valid topic for discussion or such data were "left out" of publications composed for public consumption. These problems render many of those early works unadaptable to this type of essay. Other, more recent efforts in the humanities and social sciences continue to mirror a great deal of misunderstanding about the Indian experience. It is, then, for these reasons we have chosen to review works by contemporary American Indians who are open about their lifestyle.

CONTEMPORARY NATIVE AMERICAN LITERATURE– IDENTIFYING ISSUES

American Indian lesbian and gay poetry and short stories reveal insight into a number of issues of importance to human service workers. Their stories lend acumen to and are helpful in understanding the Indian clients' needs from within their unique person-in-situation fit. The issues chosen for this article are derived from life experiences and as such they blend the social and personal.

On the social level are the Indians' encounters with cultural miscommunication and misunderstanding which, unfortunately, are common experiences when they live in non-Indian environments. The effects of these experiences are greatly determined by the presence of an American Indian community, and the quality of support it provides to the individual. On the personal level are intra-couple conflicts that arise from relationships with non-Indian lovers, problems involving substance abuse, and "homelessness," which is a disparaging reality for many Indians and which is often experienced on both the physical and spiritual planes.

Each of these topics is interwoven into the works of many heterosexual American Indian writers and artists. A common theme found throughout both American Indian lesbian and gay writings, and the works of other Indian writers is substance abuse, primarily alcohol. Pulitzer Prize winning American Indian writers N. Scott Momaday (Kiowa-Cherokee), Simon Ortiz (Acoma Pueblo), James Welch (Blackfoot-Gros Ventre), and Louise Erdrich (Chippewa, German-American), to mention a few, all depict the struggle of American Indians attempting to overcome the longest lasting plague brought to this continent by Western civilization.

Some of the literature centers on the introduction of alcohol during the "first contact" with Europeans. In *A National Disgrace,* Lawrence William O'Conner (Winnebago) (1988, p. 128) wrote, "The Indians occupied land white people wanted, and the whites did everything possible to remove them from their land. Disease, decay and alcoholism were introduced among the native people." A similar observation is found in *Understanding Grandfather,* a poem written by Daniel Little Hawk (1988, p. 193) (Lakota/Southern Cheyenne/Aztec). In this piece, the grandfather tells how things have changed since his youth,

> . . . our young men spend their time drinking whiskey, fighting each other, and shaming our people . . . this is not how we were meant to spend our days. The *wasicun* do not speak the truth. Their tongues are always forked. They stole our land, our ponies, our way of life and killed the buffalo and our self-respect. (Italics added)

Both of these citations demonstrate the confusion and pain that over the centuries have become integrated into the psyche of the modern Indian. The history of their ancestors is a bittersweet memory and their lessons are cherished as the younger generations struggle to gain equilibrium in an alien world which has been thrust upon them. Maintaining the tradition of teaching through oral history, the twentieth century Indians also use the printed media to continue the transmittal of life-wisdom to their youth. Many of these contemporary poets and writers often convey the bitter-sweet essence of their lives spent in an alien world. Their works are intricate weavings which interlace ancestral tradition with comtemporay social issues.

Gay and Lesbian Bars

While many writers chose to recount the historical development of the epidemic of alcohol, others relate accounts of current drinking behaviors to remind themselves and others of the continuing debilitation they have suffered for over 500 years. A common setting for the modern experience is the cultural phenomena of the "Indian bar" as well as the "gay bar" in gay and lesbian American Indian literature.

Joy Harjo (Creek) (1983, p. 21) gives a description of an Indian bar in her poem *Night Out*:

> You are the one who slapped Anna on the back,
> > told her to drink up
> > that it didn't matter anyway.
> You poured Jessie another Coors, and another one
> > > > and another.
> It doesn't end
> For you are multiplied by drinkers, by tables, by jukeboxes
> > > by bars.
> You are the circle of lost ones
> > > our relatives.
> You have paid the cover charge thousands of times over
> with your lives
> > > and now you are afraid
> > > you can never get out.

Paula Gunn Allen (Laguna/Sioux) writes about the turbulent life of a Cheyenne lesbian named Allie. Allie comes out in the army where she is introduced to her first gay bar. "There was a community of lesbians, of sorts, that had grown up around their army days' bar, the Silver Slipper, a lesbian tavern that was discreetly tucked away on the second floor of one of the downtown buildings" (Allen, 1988, pp. 140-141).

Maurice Kenny (Mohawk) (1979, p. 37), again using the scene of a gay bar, juxtaposes traditional and contemporary images in his poem, *Comanche of the Yamaha:*

> Comanche scout feathered and painted
> eager to war Oakland
> hotels and smoky barrooms
> eager to strike coup on some head
> who kneels to lance
> and the touch of soft Comanche hands.

Both writers, Kenny and Allen, describe without imposing value judgments, the setting where gay and lesbian Indian people go to socialize. Harjo's poem injects an essence of lamentation for the valuable lives that have been lost while in search of relief from the pain inflicted by poverty, discrimination, and feelings of hopelessness that are all too often part of being Indian.

While intoxication and its eventual development into alcoholism are often mentioned, these situations are not always present in many Native Indian literary works. However, these incapacitating addictions are not to be thought of as unimportant issues to Native American gays and lesbians. For many of them periodically fight bouts of addiction and alcoholism, not just throughout their own lives but through the lives of those close to them.

Understanding the Issues

As mentioned previously, the reader must not misconstrue the magnitude of substance abuse present in the gay or lesbian Indian community nor must it be construed as symptomatic of the subculture. The general American Indian population suffers from the same abuses as well, and there are no available overall statistics of drinking behaviors in American Indian gay and lesbian groups. There is, however, evidence of serious negative trends found in the general Indian population. For example, fetal alcohol syndrome is 33 times higher among Native Americans than among Euro-Americans

(Chavez, Cordero, & Becerra, 1989). Additionally, over 80% of homicides, suicides and auto crashes involving Indians are alcohol-related (Smith, 1989), which contributes, in no small way to the average life-expectancy for an American Indian, which is twenty-five years below that of the national average for other ethnicities living in the U.S. (O'Conner, 1988, p. 129).

The issue of alcohol abuse is relevant to many peoples world-wide as well as to the lesbian and gay American Indian subcultures. However, because alcohol abuse may be symptomatic of deeper psychological issues, some of which are mentioned in this paper, it is important that the social service worker be aware of the specific cultural aspects involved. The worker must be sensitive to the special needs of his or her Indian clients and must also be knowledge-able of the appropriate local Native American agencies and support groups that provide services based on cultural models specific to American Indian populations. In locations that do not have an American Indian unit existing in the social and human services agencies, this may require some effort on the part of the service provider to locate such groups. However, the effort is well worth the outcome. Another cultural aspect which has become a social issue among human service providers is the itinerant lifestyle of many Indians who have left homes and reservations.

Homelessness

We have chosen the word homelessness to describe a condition found in the works of gay and lesbian Native American authors. "Wandering" would be a more appropriate term, as many American Indians move from place to place in no particular pattern, often searching for, and not finding, viable prospects for work or housing. Maurice Kenny's *Yuchi Brave* (1979, p. 28), states:

> Oklahoma Dust
> your father paints your liquid vision
> in the alleys of San Francisco
> where you wander with wet voices

This condition of "wandering" is common to the American Indian community and is not seen as a negative social phenomena. It is therefore important for social service workers to examine this issue in the context of the evolution of American Indian history.

Many tribes have histories of migrations, even those who lived in established cities such as the groups commonly referred to in the American southwest as the Pueblos of Arizona and New Mexico, as well as numerous other tribes living in what is now Canada, Mexico and the U.S. Bands and tribes migrated with the seasons across lands that had no state or international boundaries imposed upon them. Archaeologists, a number of whom are Native Americans, have documented a myriad of permanent, seasonal, and hunting campsites throughout these three countries that indicate the existence of a highly sophisticated network of migration and trade routes established by this continent's original inhabitants. It was not until the late 1800s and the early 1900s, that the U.S. government began imposing "forced" moves from the Indian's traditional territories to forts and later reservations. A Native American of those times had no concept of homelessness.

Boarding Schools

Through the 1800s and into the 1940s the federal government instituted the American Indian boarding school system. Children were removed (often forcibly) from their homes, families and reservations to far away cities. This was the beginning of Indian homelessness, when the first child was taken to places like Riverside, California or Santa Fe, New Mexico and forced to live among people to whom she or he could neither relate nor understand. These strangers included not only the Europeans but also other Indian children who, having been gathered from every corner of the country and deposited in these institutions, rarely spoke the same language, knew the same customs or shared the same childhood memories.

Relocation Programs

The last aspect important to the understanding of the Indian's non-sedentary history is the government policy referred to as "relocation." Instituted in the 1950s and 1970s, reservation Indians were given opportunities to move to large urban centers such as Los Angeles, Minneapolis or Chicago. Large numbers of tribal members moved away from families in hopes of finding work and housing both of which were sadly lacking on the reservations. It may have been during this period that the practice of "wandering" between reservation land and urban centers was born (Churchill, 1993; Duran, Guillory, & Tingley, 1994; Olsen & Wilson, 1984; Weeks, 1988).

Cross-Cultural Misunderstanding and Cultural Discontinuity

The themes of cross-cultural disparity are prevalent in gay and lesbian Indian writings. The romanticized images of American Indian peoples have been instituted and perpetuated by the dominant society for the last 500 years. In his article, *Indians on the Shelf,* Michael Dorris (Modoc) (1987, p. 99) explains how these perceptions work,

> For most people, the myth has become real and a preferred substitute for ethnographic reality. The Indian mystique was designed for mass consumption by a European audience . . . [i]t is little wonder then, that many non-Indians literally would not know a real Native American if they fell over one, for they have been prepared for a well-defined, carefully honed legend.

If non-Indian social workers are insensitive to this issue they can unknowingly exacerbate the situation as well as discourage the client from seeking help. For instance, American Indians vary greatly in their physical appearances. An Indian who doesn't fit the stereotyped, romanticized image is often insulted with statements such as, "You're not really Indian, are you?" or, "So, you're part Indian?"

The following account provides an example of this type of insensitivity. A light-skinned Indian woman recently went to a gay community service center to inquire about obtaining space and time for an American Indian rap (discussion) group. Although the gay white male service worker conveyed a generally positive attitude, he ended their conversation saying, "You aren't really Indian, are you?" Even though insulted, the woman was polite and took a brief moment to educate him on Indians and the variances of skin color. Although she was able to shake off this insensitive remark, she finally decided to hold her group meetings elsewhere (Personal communication, 1995).

Service providers and workers need to be aware of cultural differences. Sometimes a worker's lack of understanding can be interpreted as insensitivity. This situation is illustrated in Daniel Little Hawk's *Understanding Grandfather* (1988, p. 194), in which a young man, whose grandfather is dying in a hospital, has his first encounter with the pain caused by the unexpected callousness of a hospital employee:

> "Times have changed, Grandfather. The whites are our friends. They respect us and our beliefs."

> "What you say may be true but I will not live long enough to see it. I hear the call of Owl Woman and the spirits of my mother and father. It is time for me to sing my death song. Remember the old ways, my son.
> When I breathe my last, remember to open the window to release my spirit to the other world. This is very important. Promise me you will do this."

> "I promise Grandfather. Is there anything else you want me to do? Grandfather? Grandfather? I never had a chance to . . . "

> "But it was my grandfather's last wish and an important ritual for our people."

> "I don't care about your superstitions. This is an air-conditioned building. We don't allow the windows open."

In the above excerpt the devaluation of traditional American Indian ways occurs at a crucial moment for the young man and he was robbed of the opportunity to fulfill his grandfather's last request. Unfortunately, the actions of the non-Indian service provider in this scenario are not new or unique. The hospital worker was probably unaware of the magnitude of the damage inflicted on the Indian youth, especially since the boy thought of himself as well integrated into and accepted by mainstream society. The boy learned a brutal lesson: Indians and their religious beliefs are seldom respected by non-Indians.

In the poem, *Her Name is Helen,* Beth Brant (Bay of Quinte Mohawk) (1988, p. 177) gives insight into cultural misunderstanding that often occurs in situations where an Indian has relationships with non-Indians. This poem relates how an Indian woman is often treated by the non-Indian lesbian community. The main character, Helen, came from Washington State twenty years ago, and now, at the age of 42, is living in Detroit, Michigan.

When she was laid off from the factory
she got a job in a bar, serving up shots and beer.
Instead of tips, she gets presents from her customers.
Little wooden statues of Indians in headdress.
Naked pictures of squaws with braided hair.
Feather roach clips in fuschia and chartreuse.
Everybody loves Helen . . .
She's had lots of girlfriends.
White women who wanted to take care of her,
who liked Indians,
who think she's a tragedy . . .

Her girlfriends took care of her.
Told her what to say
how to act more like an Indian.
You should be proud of your Indian heritage.
Wear more jewelry.
Go to the Indian Center.

This is an example of society's need to make Indians fit romanticized models. The non-Indian lesbian girlfriends unreservedly tell Helen what Indians are and how they should look, act, and dress. Helen is taught to be the kind of Indian her non-Indian lesbian friends want her to be.

Experiences of the gay male Indian are not much different than those of Helen. Concerning the dilemmas of having non-Indian lovers, in his poem, *Santa Fe, New Mexico,* Maurice Kenny (1979, pp. 14-15) wryly comments:

Underground
toilets
in plush
hotels
frighten
Yaquis
looking for a quick lay
on the tour
of toilets;
only place
in town
where an Indian
can touch
an Irishman . . .
and keep
his Sacred
Mountains . . .

In Kenny's example, the feelings associated with the conquest of non-Indians in sexual relationships are dampened with the reminder that it is only within this limited context that the Indian can gain any semblance of equality in relationships with the European-American and still maintain his Indian identity. He does this by portraying the romanticized role of Indian as defined by " . . . the Chamber of Commerce" (Kenny, 1979, p. 14), which prefers the more quaint image of him as seller of Indian jewelry to tourists.

Other writers, such as Paula Gunn Allen, explore the contradictory nature of an American Indian lesbian trying to persevere in a European lesbian clique. Her short story, *Deep Purple* (Allen, 1989), describes the experience of Leela, a Native American lesbian who attends group counseling meetings with her liberal Euro-American lover. The story makes a point of showing how these meetings affect a woman of color. Primarily designed to address issues in Western cultural and psychological terms, the counseling sessions deny Leela access to Indian ways of healing. Leela states, "If Maggie had been a traditional, I could have gone to the medicine woman or someone and talked about this" (Allen, 1989, p. 244).

In addition to cultural awareness, the social service provider must also develop an understanding of their clients' personal and social environment. Simply being American Indian does not guarantee that a person will associate with or have lovers who are of the same tribe or ethnicity. This pattern of relationships holds especially true in the urban setting. For example, a study conducted by Grandbois and Schadt (1994) examined the connection between social isolation and alienation among American Indians residing in urban areas. They found that a positive correlation exists between the number of years an Indian woman resides in an urban area and the degree of social isolation she experiences. Rather than becoming increasingly assimilated into the urban lifestyle, many American Indians experience disaffection. The overwhelming loneliness experienced by one Native American woman who was unable to blend the Western and Indian worldviews is poignantly depicted in Joy Harjo's (1988) *The Woman Hanging from the Thirteenth Floor Window:*

> She thinks of all the women she has been, of all
> the men. She thinks of the color of her skin, and
> of Chicago streets, and of waterfalls and pines.
> She thinks of moonlight nights, and of cool spring storms.
> Her mind chatters like neon and northside bars.
> She thinks of the 4 a.m. lonelinesses that have folded
> her up like death, discordant, without logical and
> beautiful conclusions. Her teeth break off at the edges.
> She would speak . . .

> And the woman hanging from the 13th floor window
> hears other voices. Some of them scream out from below
> for her to jump, they would push her over. Others cry softly
> from the sidewalks, pull their children up like flowers and
>   gather
> them into their arms. They would help her, like themselves.

> But she is the woman hanging from the 13th floor window,
> and she knows she is hanging by her own fingers, her
> own skin, her own thread of indecision.

This poem illustrates an American Indian's experience of the concept of cultural discontinuity presented by anthropologist John Ogbu (1982). Although he formulated this theory to apply to Native Americans in the Western educational system, his observations also hold true in the social arena. According to Ogbu, discontinuity takes place when there is a lack of congruence between dominant society's values and the Indians' traditional values of home and community.

This lack of consistency between worldviews not only creates confusion and disorientation for many urban Indians, it is further magnified by the deprivation of significant others and the support of the clan and tribe members. Already isolated from mainstream society, the urban-dwelling American Indian is severed from the support of his or her extended family and social/spiritual support networks, engulfed in a society that does not pay heed to the needs of the individual (Reyhner, 1992).

Respect is another key to the philosophy of traditional Native American values. Emma Widmark (Tlingit), who is a Past Grand President of the Alaska Native Sisterhood, has defined respect as recognizing that people have " . . . good reason for believing the way they believe, whether we agree or not" (Demmert, 1983, p. 44). In addition to respect, she includes honor, service in the form of generosity, sacrifice of personal goals for the betterment of the community, and finally, spirituality, which she stated is " . . . probably the greatest overriding value . . . of who we are" (Demmert, 1983, p. 45).

The record has shown that efforts to eradicate Native American identity by replacing it with that of the dominant culture serves only to alienate Indian students and put them in the unnecessary position of having to choose one over the other (Wright, 1996). "Neither choice is desirable or necessary" (Reyhner, 1992, p. 53).

Cultural Discontinuity in the Lesbian and Gay American Indian Community

The positive environment an American Indian community can provide for its gay and lesbian members can not be understated whether it be the comfort of an American Indian lover or the security provided by a traditional Native American community. Maurice

Kenny has written poems about the comfort of Indian lovers and traditional Indian values. His many poems have described encounters with Apache, Papago, Yuchi, Comanche, Yaqui, and Navajo men. These poems are sensuous tributes filled with wit and irony of the comfort provided by men of many indigenous nations. He writes:

> Apache who struck coup on a Mohawk
> and left the bed victorious. (Kenny 1979, p. 17)

One of Kenny's often published poems, *Winkte,* is a tribute to the special status attributed to an alternative gendered person (see Brown, this volume). This *Winkte* (Lakota Sioux word for homosexual male), is comparable to the Navajo *nagleeh* (one with special skills). Many contemporary Indian gays and lesbians look to these people as their forbears and celebrate their special status in the American Indian community. Kenny's *Winkte* (1979, p. 11) reflects the loss of the tribal esteem and respect that was once afforded to the other gendered people among the American Indians,

> We were special to the Sioux, Cheyenne, Ponca
> And the Crow who valued our worth and did not spit
> Names at our lifted skirts nor kicked our nakedness.
> We had power with the people!

Other Indian authors have also written about gay or lesbian American Indian encounters in a more folkloric manner. Daniel-Harry Steward (Wintu) (1988, pp. 157-162) wrote a beautiful short story about the sacred yet mundane encounter in *Coyote and Tehoma*. In this story, the two supernatural beings have a same-gender relationship which never ends; it merely takes a different form.

> You are a God who became a man,
> Said crow to Coyote,
> and Tehoma was a man who became a God.
> He could not have done as you have done.
> So his spirit has been changed into the stars,
> And at edge of twilight you can hear Coyote
> Calling for his lover who waits above
> In the starry starry night.

A significant number of studies have found that alternative gen-dered persons have historically been accepted in many American Indian tribes (Grahn, 1984; Greenberg, 1986; Roscoe, 1987). Each of these studies also notes the decline in this traditional acceptance. Some researchers feel that Christian values, introduced and often inflicted upon indigenous people during the boarding school era, are responsible for this rejection (Grahn, 1984; Greenberg, 1986).

Understanding a client is not always an easy task. It is much simpler to classify people into either an "American Indian" or "gay" category, thinking that either label will sufficiently describe an individual. As we have seen from the literary works presented here, gay and lesbian American Indians are unique and not readily classifiable. Through our survey of openly gay and lesbian Native American writers we have found a number of themes common to the Indian experience. Problems with alcohol, homelessness, cultur-al miscommunication and misunderstandings, conflicts with non-Indian lovers and the availability and quality of an American Indian support system are all inextricably interwoven into the reality of the individual. Social service workers need to be aware of the history, spirituality, and current situation of American Indian people.

Today there is an overwhelming call for a return to traditional American Indian values. Contemporary gay and lesbian American Indians feel this summons should be heeded.

REFERENCES

Allen, P.G. (1989). Deep purple. In P.G. Allen (Ed.), *Spider woman's granddaugh-ters* (pp. 229-244). New York, NY: Fawcett Columbine.

Allen, P.G. (1988). Raven's road. In W. Roscoe (Ed.), *Living the spirit: A gay American Indian anthology* (pp. 134-152). New York, NY: St. Martin's Press.

Brant, B. (1988). Her name is Helen. In W. Roscoe (Ed.), *Living the spirit: A gay American Indian anthology* (pp. 176-179). New York, NY: St. Martin's Press.

Chavez, G., Cordero, J., & Beccera, J. (1989). Leading major congenital mal-formations among minority groups in the United States. *Journal of the Ameri-can Medical Association, 261* (2), 205-209.

Churchill, W. (1993). *Struggle for the land.* Monroe, ME: Common Courage Press.

Demmert, W.G. (Ed.) (1985). *A Southeastern conference on Native education.* Juneau, AK: University of Alaska.

Dorris, M. (1987). Indians on the shelf. In C. Martin (Ed.), *The American Indian and the problem of history* (pp. 98-113). New York, NY: Oxford University Press.

Duran, E., Guillory, B., & Tingley, P. (1994, January). *Domestic violence in Native American communities: The effects of intergenerational post traumatic stress.* Paper presented at the meeting of the Mental Wellness Workshop, Los Angeles, CA.

Erdrich, L. (1984). *Love medicine.* New York, NY: Bantam Books.

Grahn, J. (1984). Strange country this: Lesbianism and North American Indian tribes. *Journal of Homosexuality, 9* (2/3), 43-57.

Grandbois, G.H., & Schadt, D. (1994). Indian identification and alienation in an urban community. *Psychological Reports, 74* (1), 211-216.

Greenberg, D.F. (1986). Why was the berdache ridiculed? *Journal of Homosexuality, 11* (1/2), 179-190.

Harjo, J. (1983). *She had some horses.* New York, NY: Thunder's Mouth Press.

Harjo, J. (1988). The woman hanging from the thirteenth floor window. In D. Niatum (Ed.), *American Indian prose & poetry.* San Francisco, CA: Harper & Row.

Jacobs, S., & Cromwell, J. (1992). Visions and revisions of reality: Reflections on sex, sexuality, gender, and gender variance. *Journal of Homosexuality, 23* (4), 43-69.

Kenny, M. (1979). *Only as far as Brooklyn.* Boston, MA: Good Gay Poets.

Little Hawk, D. (1988). Understanding grandfather. In W. Roscoe (Ed.), *Living the spirit: A gay American Indian anthology* (pp. 193-194). New York, NY: St. Martin's Press.

Momaday, N.S. (1989). *House made of dawn.* New York, NY: Harper & Row Publishers, Inc.

O'Conner, L.W. (1988). A national disgrace. In W. Roscoe (Ed.), *Living the spirit: A gay American Indian anthology* (pp. 128-130). New York, NY: St. Martin's Press.

Ogbu, J. (1982). Cultural discontinuities and schooling. *Anthropology and Education Quarterly, 13* (4), 244.

Olsen, J.S., & Wilson, R. (1984). *Native Americans in the twentieth century.* Urbana, IL: University of Illinois Press.

Ortiz, S. (1976). A barroom fragment. In *Going for the rain.* New York, NY: Harper & Row Publishers, Inc.

Prather, K. (1988). Becoming Indian. In W. Roscoe (Ed.), *Living the spirit: A gay American Indian anthology* (pp. 119-127). New York, NY: St. Martin's Press.

Reyhner, J. (1992). American Indians out of school: A review of school-based causes and solutions. *Journal of American Indian Education, 31* (3), 37-56.

Roscoe, W. (1987). Bibliography of berdache and alternative gender roles among North American Indians. *Journal of Homosexuality, 14* (3-4), pp. 81-171.

Smith, E.M. (1989). Services for Native Americans. *Alcohol Health and Research World, 13* (1), 94.

Steward, D.H. (1988). Coyote and Tehoma. In W. Roscoe (Ed.), *Living the spirit: A gay American Indian anthology* (pp. 157-162). New York, NY: St. Martin's Press.

Weeks, P. (1988). *1542 to the present: The American Indian experience, a profile.* Arlington Heights, IL: Forum Press, Inc.

Welch, J. (1988). Winter in the blood. In, A.R. Velie (Ed.), *American Indian literature: An anthology* (pp. 315-335). Norman, OK: University of Oklahoma Press.

Welch, J. (1976). Getting things straight. In *Riding the earthboy 40.* New York, NY: Harper & Row Publishers, Inc.

Welch, J. (1976). Harlem, Montana: Just off the reservation. In *Riding the earthboy 40.* New York, NY: Harper & Row Publishers, Inc.

Wright, J.A. (1996). *Native American Indians in higher education.* Unpublished master's thesis, California State University, Long Beach, CA.

Developing AIDS Services
for Native Americans:
Rural and Urban Contrasts

Ron Rowell

SUMMARY. As the number of Native American people with HIV infection continues to grow, the need to develop services that are

Ron Rowell, MPH, is a citizen of the Choctaw Nation of Oklahoma, of Choctaw and Kaskaskia Indian descent. He is a founder and Executive Director of the National Native American AIDS Prevention Center in Oakland, CA. He received his master's degree in public health from the University of California at Berkeley in 1978. He sits on the Editorial Board of the professional journal "Current Issues in Public Health," and on the editorial advisory committee of "AIDS in the World," an annual publication of the Francois-Xavier Bagnoud Institute on Health and Human Rights at Harvard University. He also sits on the Board of Directors of the Friendship House Association of American Indians in San Francisco.

Address correspondence to Ron Rowell, MPH, NNAAPC, 2100 Lakeshore Avenue, Suite A, Oakland, CA 94606.

[Haworth co-indexing entry note]: "Developing AIDS Services for Native Americans: Rural and Urban Contrasts." Rowell, Ron. Co-published simultaneously in *Journal of Gay & Lesbian Social Services* (The Haworth Press, Inc.) Vol. 6, No. 2, 1997, pp. 85-95; and: *Two Spirit People: American Indian Lesbian Women and Gay Men* (ed: Lester B. Brown) The Haworth Press, Inc., 1997, pp. 85-95; and: *Two Spirit People: American Indian Lesbian Women and Gay Men* (ed: Lester B. Brown) Harrington Park Press, an imprint of The Haworth Press, Inc., 1997, pp. 85-95. Single or multiple copies of this article are available for a fee from The Haworth Document Delivery Service [1-800-342-9678, 9:00 a.m. - 5:00 p.m. (EST). E-mail address: getinfo@haworth.com].

tailored to the special needs of rural/reservation and urban Native Americans grows with it. The experiences of AIDS programs in two very different sites, one on the Navajo Reservation in Arizona and another in New York City, illustrate both similarities and differences in the needs of clients. Barriers that prevent or discourage access to care for Native American people living with HIV/AIDS exist in both places, but it is in the specifics that tailored solutions are clearly required. Native American AIDS activists have been working hard to meet the needs of Native Americans living with HIV/AIDS and their progress is encouraging. *[Article copies available for a fee from The Haworth Document Delivery Service: 1-800-342-9678. E-mail address: getinfo @ haworth.com]*

When comparisons are made between the numbers of reported cases of AIDS among American Indians and Alaska Natives (Native American) and other ethnic groups in the U.S., some people respond with a shrug. Why should Native Americans be so concerned with what appear to be relatively low numbers of diagnosed cases of AIDS? The reasons are historical and based upon our current knowledge of other health problems.

First, infectious disease epidemics were responsible for the deaths of perhaps 12-15 million indigenous Americans after 1492 (Thornton, 1987). Whole cultures were decimated by such epidemics as smallpox, tuberculosis, syphilis, influenza and others. In fact, tuberculosis continued well into the mid-twentieth century to kill Native Americans at a rate far surpassing that of most other Americans. This history is therefore alive in the consciousness of many Native people. A threat of the magnitude of the AIDS pandemic immediately raises the specter of another holocaust like that experienced by our ancestors.

Second, it is an unfortunate fact that the health status of Native people is lower on virtually every indicator than the U.S. population as a whole (OTA, 1986). The latest studies available on primary and secondary syphilis, gonorrhea and chlamydia among Native Americans showed rates that averaged twice as high as in the rest of the population and in some states ten times as high (Toomey, Oberschelp, & Greenspan, 1989). Alcohol and drug abuse accounts for the majority of the causes of mortality and close to four out of ten Native American people die before the age of 45.

The distribution of Native American AIDS cases has changed very little since reporting began. The majority of cases are among men (85%) and among men, gay/bisexual men account for seventy-nine percent (79%) of the cases. One significant difference between Native American AIDS cases and those of all other ethnic groups is the relatively higher proportion of gay/bisexual men who also use drugs intravenously (17%). It is not clear what accounts for this. Research on American Indian health in general and AIDS in particular is scarce.

There is a higher proportion of women in the Native American AIDS population than in that of White/Non-Hispanics. This parallels the experience of Hispanics and African-Americans and can be attributed overwhelmingly to the uninvestigated and generally unrecognized problem of intravenous drug use in our population. Seventeen pediatric Native American cases have been reported, of whom ten were a result of intravenous drug use by the mother or sex with an injection drug user (IDU). The study published in 1992 by the Centers for Disease Control and Prevention and the Indian Health Service reported the results of a national blinded seroprevalence survey of rural pre-natal clinics. They found that infection rates among rural Native American women in their third trimester of pregnancy were from four to eight times higher than rates found among other rural women in similar studies (Conway, Ambrose, Epstein, Chase, Johannes, Hooper, & Helgerson, 1992).

There has been an ongoing concern within the Native American community that the actual number of Native American AIDS cases is underreported. Studies by the CDC in Los Angeles, California, and Seattle, Washington (reported in 1992) confirm that in those two cities at least, Native American AIDS cases were misreported as White or Hispanic in 50%-75% of the cases (Hurlich, Hopkins, Sakuma, & Conway, 1992; Lieb, Kerndt, Hedderman, Chase, Yao, & Conway, 1989). Misreporting of race/ethnicity is an old problem in Native American epidemiology and is the result of a population that is now by and large of mixed racial heritage—and has been since 1930 (Thornton, 1987).

The response of Native American communities across the U.S. and Canada has been mixed. From a handful of prevention education efforts in 1988 there are now over one hundred in every region of the U.S. and at least twelve HIV case management programs. The National Native American AIDS Prevention Center (NNAAPC) was organized in 1987 in response to the reluctance at that time of national Native American health agencies to engage the issue. The establishment of an AIDS-specific national Native American organization made it possible to focus the energy required to organize both on a national level as well as within the 500+ Native tribes and villages of the U.S. In Canada there are now aboriginal (as we are termed in Canadian English) AIDS projects in the provinces of British Columbia, Alberta, Ontario and Nova Scotia, due almost entirely to the efforts of two-spirit (gay/lesbian) people. NNAAPC applied for and was awarded funding from the Centers for Disease Control and Prevention in 1988 to provide training, technical assistance and information services to Native communities. In 1989, NNAAPC organized the National Indian AIDS Media Consortium, a partnership of Native American newspapers, magazines, newsletters, and radio stations or syndicated radio programs to keep the issue of HIV/AIDS alive before the Native American public. NNAAPC embarked upon a national project to develop Native two-spirit leadership in HIV prevention in 1995.

In 1991 the National Native American AIDS Prevention Center applied for and was awarded a grant from the Health Resources and Services Administration with funds from the Ryan White Care Act's "Special Projects of National Significance" provisions, to develop a case management demonstration project for Native Americans living in the state of Oklahoma and on the Tohono O'odham and Pascua Yaqui Reservations, including the Tucson metropolitan area of Arizona. In 1994 this free-standing case management model was replicated in ten sites throughout the U.S., including the state of Hawaii, Seattle, the Chugach region of Alaska, New York City, Robeson County, North Carolina, Milwaukee, Minneapolis, Kansas City, the Navajo Nation and Phoenix. In addition, funds went to support a developing organization of Native American people with AIDS, "Positively Native," and traditional medicine support and consultation to the national case management sites based in rural San Diego County, California. The Navajo Nation and New York City sites illustrate some of the issues faced by Native American clients in two very different environments.

AIDS INTERVENTION IN TWO SITES

Arizona

The Navajo Nation AIDS Network, founded in 1990, is located in a trailer parked in the dusty lot of the Chinle Community Center in Chinle, Arizona, near the Canyon de Chelly. Melvin Harrison, Director of the program, founded it in order to develop a Navajo-specific response to the epidemic and to improve care for people living with HIV/AIDS on the reservation.

According to Harrison (Harrison, personal communication, January 17, 1995) the Navajo Nation is generally homophobic and as a result, people have a difficult time coming out of the closet. There are places on the reservation where this is not so, especially among traditional elders, but among younger people there is a lot of ridicule and intimidation. There have been some reports of violence against gay men in particular. He says seventy to eighty percent of the time people will oppose having two-spirits present to speak at AIDS conferences on the reservation. He thinks that as more elders become involved in the effort, that might change. Younger gay Navajos think of AIDS as a problem only of older gay men or of urban Indians, not something that affects rural/reservation younger people. He says, too, that many bisexual men go to urban areas to have sex with other men and return to the reservation. Unlike a few years ago, Navajos are now infecting other Navajos.

Beginning in 1988 until 1992 Harrison worked with a voluntary effort at Chinle called the Central Navajo AIDS Coalition (CNAC) with three or four other people. One of these people was a two-spirit. The CNAC was focused on prevention, offering education to a wide variety of people on the reservation from kindergarten age to elders. Harrison worked with people living with AIDS all of whom were closeted and all of whom have now passed on. However, the CNAC was working only in the Chinle Agency, the smallest of these subdivisions of the nation. People in other parts of the Navajo Nation expressed a strong desire to see an AIDS program that would focus on the Nation as a whole.

In April, 1990, Harrison advertised a meeting to establish such an agency and 35 people attended, among whom were at least two two-spirit people who have remained involved. The Navajo AIDS

Network (NAN), a non-profit agency organized under both Navajo and Arizona law, continues the work of HIV prevention education, and HIV in the workplace education. NAN also sponsors the annual Navajo AIDS Conference. It now also provides case management services for 10-12 Navajos living with HIV/AIDS.

The issues for a "typical" PWA on the Navajo reservation, according to Harrison, are first and foremost related to confidentiality. For this reason PWAs will often not seek care through the Indian Health Service facility or through the tribal health department. He says that clients "test them out" for a while before deciding whether to seek services at NAN to insure that they can keep the client's confidentiality. Often the issue is compounded because they are also hiding their same-sex sexual orientation. A typical client has problems with drug and alcohol addiction that Harrison believes could be related to the stress of living in the closet.

Because clients don't want to seek care locally, medical services become a problem. Navajos living on the reservations are expected to seek care at an Indian Health Service (IHS) or tribal facility on the reservation. If they go off the reservation for care, IHS will not pay for it unless they have referred the client. Thus clients are expected to pay for their own care when self-referring off-reservation, a problem for a predominantly poor population.

Transportation is also a serious problem. The Navajo Nation is quite large in area and for clients who do not live close to a main highway, bad weather may make the dirt tracks impassable. Some clients don't have access to automobiles. Housing is also a challenge, especially for clients who may have to travel many miles to an IHS facility on the reservation and need somewhere to stay while undergoing tests or a series of examinations, and who may need someone to check up on them often. Some Navajo government departments have not been especially sensitive to the needs of people living with AIDS. For those out of the closet who use the IHS hospital, a major concern is the waiting time even when they have appointments. This waiting time is typically two to four hours on average. A recent client spent the entire day in the waiting room.

NAN's program was supported during FY 1995 with $52,000 from the National Native American AIDS Prevention Center with funds provided by the Health Resources and Services Administration. The Navajo Nation government has contributed $50,000 and additional small sums are earned from assorted small consulting contracts, fundraising dances and poster sales.

New York

Native Americans living with HIV/AIDS in New York City face different challenges according to HIV case managers at New York City's urban Native American center (D. Gubiseh-Ayala, personal communication, January 18, 1995). The American Indian Community House (AICH) is located across from the Joseph Papp Shakespeare Theater in Soho, a block east of Broadway. The only canyons are ones overhung with glass and concrete. AICH began its HIV/AIDS project in 1990, organized by Curtis Harris and a couple of colleagues working in the substance abuse program at the time. Community members infected with HIV began showing up in their offices to ask for assistance, people who had no other options than to rely upon their own community. As a result of this, AICH decided to do a community needs assessment to understand better how to be of service to these clients. Part of that experience was learning what kinds of service networks were available in the city. It became clear that simply replicating models of services that had been developed for other populations in New York City would be ineffective for these clients. Staff heard complaints from gay Native men who had sought assistance elsewhere who were discomfited by what they perceived as callous and arrogant treatment. They reported that such treatment by AIDS services providers added to their stress because they perceived it as a lack of respect. In Native American cultures it is generally true that informality and humor are valued highly in human relationships. Euro-American folkways can feel harsh and uncaring to Native Americans reared in a Native environment.

The findings of the assessment indicated the need for a program that could offer outreach to those affected and infected, provide referrals and offer case management services. The design and implementation of these services were based upon the experience of AICH staff's work with American Indians in New York City and the need to evaluate the national case management model (referred to as the "Ahalaya case management model") developed in Oklahoma.

The program is currently seeing 22 clients living with HIV or AIDS. One of the major issues with AICH's clients is dual or multiple diagnosis. Many clients living with HIV or AIDS may also have substance addictions, as well as active tuberculosis. So many American Indians, whether they were TB infected as children on the reservations, or as adults in prison or hospital settings, are at high risk for reactivation of the primary TB infection if they are HIV+ or living with AIDS. Single room occupancies or shelters, where homeless clients are placed until permanent residence can be obtained, are rife with tuberculosis infestation.

Recent budget cuts at the Department of AIDS Services (DAS) for the City of New York have had a strong impact upon the delivery of services. According to the case manager for the program, Diana Gubiseh-Ayala (personal communication, January 18, 1995), negotiation skills are all-important for getting clients' needs met through the system. All over New York City clients of all ethnicities are finding difficulty getting services. There is no consistency or stability for the client. DAS case workers are shuffled from one office to another and their phone numbers are constantly changing so it is difficult to reach them. This causes longer delays to the already slow process of case service planning. For example, if a client is awaiting an approval for an exception to policy and it has already taken six weeks to put the paperwork together and the decision-making period goes beyond the usual four to six weeks, it can be enormously stressful to a client. It is now taking two to three months for such decisions. What do clients do if they don't have shelter? How does the case worker prevent substance abuse relapse with that kind of stress?

One of the AICH case manager's functions is to act as a housing broker, hitting the streets trying to find shelter. In Gubiseh-Ayala's opinion the case managers at DAS are not given cultural-sensitivity training. This is a significant problem. She also finds that when clients come to AICH with benefits already in place, they often are not receiving the minimum to which they are entitled. Intake assessments always include an assessment of amounts and sources of client income. The typical client at AICH is on public assistance. Occasionally a client is homeless. Clients are predominantly male and 65% are gay men. At the beginning, clients were predominantly heterosexual intravenous drug users. A significant proportion of the gay Native men being seen in the program, however, also have a history of intravenous drug use.

Often gay Native clients at AICH have not been reared in traditional ways and find it confusing to be confronted with acceptance and information supporting traditional roles for two-spirit people instead of hostility. Curtis Harris, Director of the HIV/AIDS program at AICH, finds it ironic that the AIDS epidemic has pushed two-spirit people to come forward and play a traditional role. It has also helped Native communities and two-spirits to rediscover and reapply what was a dying tradition under the onslaught of missionary ideology. He cautions that acceptance also implied a responsibility to contribute back to the community and care-giving was one of the major ways two-spirits were expected to contribute.

Access to medical care is not as much an issue for Native Americans in New York City where, according to Harris, hospitals range from excellent to fair in their ability to care for people with AIDS. One sharp contrast with the Navajo Nation, however, is the number of clients who moved to New York and became involved in the sex industry. The concept of a sex "industry" is foreign to Native Americans living in a rural/reservation setting. The organized structure of employment that exists in cities like New York does not exist on reservations, though people may work on a free-lance basis or trade sex for alcohol and drugs.

For Native Americans with HIV living in New York who are eligible for treatment through the Indian Health Service, the choice must often be made whether to return to their tribal area in order to be able to access services. This presents difficulties since some IHS facilities do not want to provide services or lack the degree of sophistication and experience of medical providers in hard-hit cities like New York. Of course, leaving close friends and a gay support network can be equally challenging.

For Native Americans with HIV/AIDS in both rural/reservation and urban settings who must rely upon IHS for care, access to common AIDS drugs has become problematic. IHS developed a national system in 1991 to provide the most common drugs to any eligible Indian being seen in any IHS-funded facility until 1993. At that time the Director of IHS decided AIDS care should be "mainstreamed" within IHS. This meant such drugs would be provided by IHS only to those Native Americans with HIV/AIDS who are eligible for contract care, effectively restricting drugs to people living on or near reservations. Other than making the majority of Native Americans ineligible for medications (only 25% of the population lives on reservations), this also throws access to AIDS drugs into competition with all other major health problems that may be covered by contract care. Typically, contract care dollars are severely limited and have seldom been able to cover the costs of care, even prior to the AIDS epidemic. An elder reminded the author at a recent meeting with the Director of IHS that on her reservation they have a saying that you should never have an auto accident between July and September because there is never funding to cover the costs of special medical needs at that point in the Federal fiscal year. She became lame as a young woman because she was not able to access contract care dollars for specialized medical care off the reservation for this reason. For those now suddenly ineligible for AIDS drugs through IHS, state Medicaid programs or the Veteran's Administration are supposed to suffice—or Native American PWAs will have to do without.

Although Native American AIDS prevention efforts and services for people living with HIV/AIDS face many challenges, both political and logistic, the commitment of Native American AIDS activists is producing results. A common thread running through much of modern Native American literature is memory: the remembrance of who we are and where we have come from in every generation as a powerful political and spiritual force. We are still here after everything, and we will continue to be here. AIDS is just another in a long line of challenges to our future and like the others, it too will be overcome.

REFERENCES

Conway, G., Ambrose, T.J., Epstein, M.R., Chase, E., Johannes, P., Hooper, E.Y., & Helgerson, S.D. (May, 1992). Prevalence of HIV and AIDS in American Indians and Alaska Natives. *The IHS Primary Care Provider, 17* (5), 65-69.

Hurlich, M.G., Hopkins, S.G., Sakuma, J., & Conway, G.A. (May, 1992). Racial ascertainment of AI/AN persons with AIDS, Seattle/King County, WA, 1980-1989. *The IHS Primary Care Provider, 17* (5), 73-75.

Lieb, L., Kerndt, P., Hedderman, M., Chase, E., Yao, J., & Conway, G. (1989). Evaluating racial classification among Native American Indians with AIDS in Los Angeles County, California. *Fifth International Conference on AIDS Abstracts # 67.*

Office of Technology Assessment, Congress of the United States. (1986). *Indian Health Care.* (DHHS Publication No. OTA-H-290). Washington, DC: U.S. Government Printing Office.

Thornton, R. (1987). *American Indian holocaust and survival: A population history since 1492.* Norman, OK: University of Oklahoma Press.

Toomey, K.T., Oberschelp, A.G., & Greenspan, J.R. (November-December, 1989). Sexually transmitted diseases and Native Americans: Trends in reported gonorrhea and syphilis morbidity, 1984-88. *Public Health Reports, 104* (6), 566-572.

AIDS Prevention
in a Rural American Indian Population:
A Collaborative Effort
Between Community and Providers

Elizabeth DePoy
Claire Bolduc

SUMMARY. This paper presents an innovative AIDS prevention program that was conducted in a rural American Indian community. The project consisted of three phases: Needs Assessment and Planning, Implementation, and Follow-Up. Through a collaborative process, project staff and community members and leaders developed and implemented culturally valued and credible sources to promote awareness of the AIDS epidemic and to reduce high-risk behavior. Following the implementation phase of the project, follow-up activities suggested that the prevention strategies were valued and effective in producing short-term responses. Further areas for improvement and the need for long-term follow-up were revealed. *[Article copies available for a fee from The Haworth Document Delivery Service: 1-800-342-9678. E-mail address: getinfo@haworth.com]*

Elizabeth DePoy, MSW, PhD, is Associate Professor, Department of Social Work, University of Maine, 103 Annex C, Orono, ME 04469. Claire Bolduc, MA, is AIDS Program Director, Central Maine Indian Association, 157 Park Street, Bangor, ME 04401.

[Haworth co-indexing entry note]: "AIDS Prevention in a Rural American Indian Population: A Collaborative Effort Between Community and Providers." DePoy, Elizabeth, and Claire Bolduc. Co-published simultaneously in *Journal of Gay & Lesbian Social Services* (The Haworth Press, Inc.) Vol. 6, No. 2, 1997, pp. 97-108; and: *Two Spirit People: American Indian Lesbian Women and Gay Men* (ed: Lester B. Brown) The Haworth Press, Inc., 1997, pp. 97-108; and: *Two Spirit People: American Indian Lesbian Women and Gay Men* (ed: Lester B. Brown) Harrington Park Press, an imprint of The Haworth Press, Inc., 1997, pp. 97-108. Single or multiple copies of this article are available for a fee from The Haworth Document Delivery Service [1-800-342-9678, 9:00 a.m. - 5:00 p.m. (EST). E-mail address: getinfo@haworth.com].

97

INTRODUCTION

As AIDS continues to seriously affect all groups of people, many efforts have been undertaken to prevent HIV transmission (Cournas, Empfield, Horwath, & Kramer, 1989). However, because the only preventive mechanisms available at the current time are behavioral (Coates, Stall, Kegeles, Lo, & McKusick, 1988), intervention strategies are limited to those which effect behavior change. Theoretically, a reduction in HIV transmission would follow from educating persons about the modes of transmission and reinforcing abstinence from behavior that places people at risk for contracting HIV. However, even though major educational efforts have been conducted nationwide, the incidence of AIDS continues to increase at alarming rates. Several studies have suggested that educational efforts may not be effective in promoting behavioral change because they are not always compatible with the cultural norms, level of knowledge and patterns of behavior of the diverse reference groups receiving the educational intervention (Des Jarlais & Friedman, 1988; Fisher, 1988; Hall, 1988). The implications of studies such as those conducted by Des Jarlais and Friedman highlight the importance of AIDS prevention programs to be culturally sensitive to their target groups and to include community members in the planning, implementation, and evaluation stages.

This paper discusses an innovative, culturally relevant AIDS prevention program which was implemented in a rural American Indian community in Central Maine. In recognition that American Indian communities hold customs and cultural norms different from those in which prevention programs previously have been conducted and documented, and furthermore that the risk behaviors in rural areas may differ significantly from those in urban areas in which the majority of programs have been implemented (Dhooper & Royse, 1989), the program planners collaborated with American Indian community members, rural community leaders and health and human service providers in planning and implementing the program.

Literature Review

Since the first documented case of AIDS in 1981 (CDC, 1988), the incidence of AIDS has doubled approximately every 8-10 months, creating a social and health problem of epidemic proportion (Batchelor, 1988). An overview of the literature and research on AIDS transmission and prevention reveals that infection with the AIDS virus is a result of behavior, not of group belongingness or serendipitous events (Stall, Coates, & Hoff, 1988; Doyle, 1988; Des Jarlais & Friedman, 1988; Peterson & Marin, 1988; Wheeler, 1989). In the absence of pharmaceutical intervention, behavior change is therefore the only prevention strategy currently available.

Many efforts aimed at reducing behaviors which place an individual at risk for contracting the AIDS virus (herein termed AIDS risk behaviors or ARB) have been initiated since the realization that AIDS has reached epidemic proportions. The majority of these efforts involve disseminating information about AIDS transmission and prevention to those at risk (Wheeler, 1989). However, research reveals equivocal findings regarding the extent to which information acquisition promotes preventive behavior. While McKusic, Horstman, and Coates (1985) found that sexual activity in a sample of gay men in San Francisco was not related to knowledge of AIDS risk behavior, Martin (1987) revealed a decline in risk behavior in gay men in New York following their exposure to AIDS information. However, neither study was able to identify the factors which could predict behavior change, although both studies acknowledged that reference group norms were important to investigate further. Des Jarlais and Friedman (1988) suggested that significant factors in the presence and continuation of ARB in a reference group include the behavioral norms and knowledge held by the group members. Interestingly, even though AIDS is a major health and social problem in some minority groups, minimal literature currently discusses prevention programs which were designed to fit with the cultural norms of those groups. The evidence pointing to the cultural group norms and beliefs as important influences on ARB suggests that social workers need to incorporate knowledge of culturally specific beliefs, norms and behaviors into their planning and implementation. Culturally relevant interventions which aim at behavior change must be developed if social workers are to be effective in promoting the reduction of ARB in culturally diverse groups.

In Maine, a predominantly rural state, there are approximately 4500 off-reservation Indians and 1300 on-reservation residents

(Central Maine Indian Association [off-reservation service agency], 1992). In the summer months, the population increases with the influx of migrant Indian blueberry pickers. Due to their unique heritage and rural location, the American Indian population holds cultural norms and customs which differ significantly from other populations in which AIDS prevention programs have been implemented. Therefore, as indicated in the literature, the special customs and structure of Indian society need to be understood by service providers in order to select prevention strategies which will be meaningful, credible and effective in preventing the spread of HIV in the American Indian population (Jacobs & Bowles, 1988).

According to Jacobs and Bowles (1988), many American Indians hold beliefs about health which are inconsistent with the medical model which has been the foundation of most AIDS education and prevention efforts. " . . . [T]he concept of health includes a sense of harmony among sociological structures and spiritual forces" (p. 97). Family structures, social roles in small rural communities and gender roles are also factors which require understanding, before a meaningful prevention program can be planned. Jacobs and Bowles (1988) also indicate that rural Indian families tend to exhibit traditional gender roles and maintain a closed community.

Unfortunately, the incidence of AIDS is increasing in the total Indian population in Maine. Currently, there are numerous reported cases of AIDS and HIV infection, and it is estimated that the majority of cases in the Indian population in Maine are unreported (Central Maine Indian Association Report, 1992). According to informants from the CMIA (Central Maine Indian Association, 1992), the major form of HIV transmission in the Indian culture is through unprotected sex. Reportedly, the predominant drug abused in the Indian culture in Maine is alcohol. The combination of unprotected sex with multiple partners and alcohol abuse has been shown to be a major risk in AIDS behavior in other populations (Stall et al., 1988). With the risk factors present and the incidence of AIDS increasing at alarming rates, the need to establish prevention programs is paramount. However, to insure the likelihood of decreasing the spread of AIDS, these programs must demonstrate collaborative planning and consistency with the cultural norms of the populations to which they are targeted.

THE PROJECT

Consistent with the literature and with sound social work practice principles, the HIV prevention project that is described herein, was specifically designed to address the unique needs, beliefs, attitudes, and risk behaviors of rural American Indians residing in Central and Northern Maine. A local agency serving the American Indian off-reservation population in Central Maine was the lead agency in the project. In order to insure adequate resources to conduct the project, the project director who worked for the lead agency successfully applied to the Office of Minority Affairs in the U.S. Department of Health and Human Services for funding support. Once funding was obtained, the project was conducted in three distinct phases: *Needs Assessment and Planning, Implementation, and Follow-Up.*

NEEDS ASSESSMENT AND PLANNING

The needs assessment and planning phase was comprised of two activities: a formal survey of AIDS risk behaviors, attitudes towards AIDS and knowledge of HIV transmission in the American Indian population in Maine and a series of collaborative planning meetings to formulate implementation strategies.

The needs research, conducted by the project director and a social work faculty member, was a paper and pencil instrument which was distributed to a convenience sample of respondents in the Native American communities in Maine. The instrument consisted of closed-ended items testing knowledge of HIV transmission, attitudes towards persons with AIDS and AIDS risk behavior. The data from 110 respondents revealed findings about AIDS knowledge, attitudes and risk behaviors that were essential in informing the planning and implementation of the project. First, the knowledge level of AIDS and HIV in the respondent group was generally high, thereby eliminating the need for major, inclusive educational efforts. However, the specific areas of needed education included HIV transmission in general, transmission between genders, and sexual prevention strategies. Interestingly, respondent misunderstandings that were illuminated in the needs assessment study seemed to be based on respondents' beliefs about HIV transmission rather than a deficit in their actual knowledge about HIV, leading the project staff to be sensitive about who they selected as transmitters of knowledge, values and attitudes related to AIDS and HIV.

Second, findings related to AIDS risk behaviors suggested that while risk behavior was relatively low in most areas, one area, that of condom use, was especially noteworthy. A significantly large group of respondents, primarily women, did not respond with the knowledge that condom use during sexual relations is a valuable prevention strategy. Further, low frequency of condom use was reported, especially by women. This phenomenon could have been a result of the traditional gender roles of women in the American Indian rural culture in that women may not have perceived themselves as the responsible party for AIDS protection. However, because IV drug use is not a major method of HIV transmission in the rural Indian population, the risk that resulted from unprotected sex was targeted as a primary part of the intervention.

The needs assessment also revealed important gender differences in the respondent group in all three areas of knowledge, attitudes, and behaviors. Male respondents held less accurate knowledge, and more conservative beliefs about AIDS and persons with AIDS, suggesting different social norms for each gender. Finally, the needs assessment did not support a significant correlation between risk behavior and either knowledge or attitudes (Depoy & Bolduc, 1992).

Once the needs assessment was completed, a special collaborative meeting was held to initiate planning. The project director, rural and American Indian community leaders and representatives, health professionals, and the university faculty member from the social work department attended the meeting. The needs assessment and other relevant information were reviewed and analyzed and synthesized with community member knowledge as a basis for formulating the overall direction for the preventive strategies. The guiding principles for the program were as follows:

1. unprotected sex seemed to be the major risk behavior that needed to be changed;
2. gender roles and cultural norms needed to be recognized in promoting condom use;

3. sources of authority and guidance needed to be credible and accepted by the target population;
4. intervention needed to include spiritual as well as biopsycho-social interventions;
5. information and values needed to be transmitted through culturally relevant and valued media.

IMPLEMENTATION

A program of multi-method interventions was implemented over a one-year period. These interventions took place in the communities of the target population to insure that a maximum number of persons would be reached. Some of the interventions were ongoing and some were time limited. Some activities were informative, while others promoted specific risk reduction behaviors and examination of values. Strategies included informative and affective as well as spiritual components.

Because the findings in the study revealed that unprotected sex was a major area of risk for the Indian population, a major emphasis was placed on safe sex. In an effort to encourage more women to demand condom use, condom jewelry was distributed. The jewelry, in the form of pins and earrings containing condoms, was fabricated by an American Indian artist to display traditional Indian design and fashion.

A second strategy to promote safe sex involved recruiting respected elders in the community to discuss safe sex with the youth in town-meeting type formats that were frequently attended to address important social and spiritual matters. Elders were also used to impart accurate information about HIV transmission, since they are considered to be a credible and valued source of knowledge in the American Indian culture.

To address other areas of concern about community knowledge, attitudes and beliefs about HIV and persons with AIDS, two types of media were employed. A theater troupe was commissioned to stage a series of plays on AIDS and HIV. The theater was selected as one culturally valued medium for presentation of sensitive issues. The scripts included information on HIV transmission, vignettes aimed at understanding the living and spiritual experience of AIDS, and messages about the responsibility of both genders to exercise safe sex.

Public announcements were also placed on local television to raise awareness of HIV and AIDS and to inform viewers about the AIDS experience. No efforts aimed specifically at imparting information about transmission and prevention over television, such as those that are typical of AIDS prevention projects, were conducted in this project because they were determined by the project leaders and the community to be irrelevant and not valued by the target population.

FOLLOW-UP

Follow-up methods for the project are still being conducted and will continue over the next year in order to determine the long-term impact of the project. To monitor the immediate impact, participants in the program and community members were asked for their input and recommendations on each interventive strategy. It appeared as if the theater and the condom jewelry were most *memorable* strategies to community members, and thus served the purpose of increasing awareness and conversation about AIDS. The extent to which this awareness translates into long-term reduction in AIDS risk behavior needs to be further explored in subsequent follow-up activity.

In order to obtain a fuller understanding of the appropriateness and impact of the program, eight project participants known to have engaged in AIDS risk behavior prior to the implementation of the project were interviewed. Three were women and five were men. All were between the ages of 20-40. Interviews were structured by seven open-ended questions exploring their knowledge of HIV transmission, their attitudes towards their own risk behavior and prevention, and their evaluation of this project for their community.

The interview data did validate the program direction in that respondents suggested that the prevention strategies were valuable in increasing community dialogue about AIDS and that the methods used were consistent with the norms and values of the rural American Indian population. For example, each of the respondents discussed spirituality as an important part of life in his/her interview and indicated that life decisions often were connected to a higher power. Three of the interviewees further indicated that AIDS prevention could best be accomplished through promoting sexual decision-making as a moral, religious responsibility. The program certainly focused on this aspect of prevention in its activities with the elders of the community and its moral messages in the theater.

Interviewees further supported the focus that the program took on condom use. Three of the men and one of the women who were interviewed each gave reasons for not using condoms even though they have sex frequently with multiple partners. For example, one man indicated that condoms decreased the pleasure from sex, while another felt that questioning his partners about their sexual history was sufficient prevention. Interestingly, each of the eight respondents was knowledgeable about signs and symptoms of AIDS, but, consistent with the sample who completed the needs assessment questionnaire, held misconceptions about transmission. Four believed that HIV could be transmitted through "bug bites," two believed that it could be transmitted through touch, and so forth. These data further confirm our original hunch regarding AIDS knowledge as myth. That is to say, it appears as if what people "know" about HIV transmission may be a function of belief, not of knowledge. This notion further supports the direction of the program, in that knowledge transmission by scientific authorities was not a viable method of intervention. Rather, the program sought to prevent HIV infection through raising awareness and changing behavior through credible, relevant strategies.

Turning attention to the media that were used, the interview data supported the appropriateness of multi-media intervention. Two of the eight respondents indicated that pamphlets written in English about HIV and AIDS were valueless because they could not read English. The television public announcements were seen and reportedly provoked thought in these two respondents.

Although condom use and moral sexual decision-making were targeted in this program, one area which was not a major focus of the program but which should be added, was the relationship among sexual decision-making, HIV, and substance use and abuse. Three of the respondents did speak at length about substance use and sexual decision-making. On the most alarming extreme, one respondent shared his apathy about AIDS and felt that while he was intoxicated, he would do nothing to diminish his pleasure, since being high was the only pleasure in his life. He therefore said that he did not care about getting or transmitting HIV as long as he could enjoy sex. On the other extreme, a female respondent said that when not intoxicated, she worried about getting AIDS, but, while intoxicated, her decision-making abilities were impaired. As a result, she has engaged in unprotected sex when using substances. These data suggest that sexual decision-making is not a unitary phenomenon and is strongly influenced by age, gender, and state of mind, particularly if someone is intoxicated. Strategies to further mediate against the alarmingly high risk of HIV transmission through sex combined with using and abusing substances should therefore be enhanced.

PRACTICE IMPLICATIONS

The project presented in this paper was an innovative prevention program which aimed to use culturally relevant and valued methods to increase awareness and decrease risk behavior. While the long-term effects of the program on these two goal areas need further investigation, the short-term follow-up activity suggests that the program was successful in the selection of strategies that were meaningful to the target community and to the participants. The project staff and community members derived valuable learning from this program, which may be helpful in informing future program development.

First, based on literature and the findings of the follow-up, it seems likely that beliefs about HIV transmission may be a cultural phenomenon, in part determined by myth and common knowledge. In this community, it was apparent that medical, scientific sources are not credible and that community members developed their own myths about transmission and prevention. In this group and possibly in others the target of change therefore must be the myths, not the transmission of scientific knowledge (Depoy & Bolduc, 1992). Furthermore, as in this project, transmitters of knowledge and value must be respected community members whose knowledge and guidance will be believed and followed by community members.

Second, this project highlighted the heterogeneity of communities and the need to approach AIDS prevention from a pluralistic perspective even within the same community. Without the television announcements, it is questionable that so many of the community members would have been reached. However, for those who do not own or value television, strategies such as the theater and town meetings were most valuable in promoting dialogue about HIV.

Third, each community has its own norms and cultural practices, particularly in rural areas where communities are not clearly visible and intact. The program discussed herein did attempt to address those norms in a sensitive and meaningful manner, in that traditional educational prevention programs were not implemented. Rather, the program activities were tailored to the special risks, beliefs and customs of the rural American Indian community. Only through engaging community leaders and members in the planning and implementation process could the program planners have gained access to the community and to the knowledge to guide the development of relevant strategies. Thus, the importance of collaboration was illuminated by this project.

Finally, only through conducting the program did needed areas for program improvement become clear. While careful and sensitive planning is an essential element of any program effort, it is insufficient by itself to insure desired outcomes. Monitoring and evaluation must be conducted as a basis for modification and improvement.

In conclusion, this paper has discussed an innovative culturally relevant project which demonstrated the value of collaborative assessment and planning. The data based program development insured that the unique norms and customs of the American Indian community were respected and integrated into all programmatic components. This project may serve to inform future program development in culturally diverse areas in which behavior change is a primary prevention strategy.

REFERENCES

Batchelor, W. (1988). AIDS 1988, the science and the limits of science. *American Psychologist, 11,* 853-858.

Centers for Disease Control. (April 11, 1988). *AIDS weekly surveillance report– United States.*

Central Maine Indian Association. (1992). Unpublished report.

Coates, T., Stall, R., Kegeles, S., Lo, B., & McKusick, L. (1988). AIDS antibody testing: Will it stop the AIDS epidemic? Will it help people infected with HIV? *American Psychologist, 11,* 859-861.

Cournas, F., Empfield, M., Horwath, E., & Kramer, M. (1989). The management of HIV infection in state psychiatry hospitals. *Hospital and Community Psychiatry, 2,* 153-157.

DePoy, E., & Bolduc, C. (1992). AIDS prevention: An empirical approach. *Journal of Multicultural Social Work, 2,* 51-78.

Des Jarlais, D., & Friedman, S. (1988). The psychology of preventing AIDS among intravenous drug users: A social learning conceptualization. *American Psychologist, 11,* 865-870.

Dhooper, S., & Royse, D. (1989). Rural attitudes about AIDS: A statewide survey. *Human Services in Rural Environments, 13,* 17-22.

Doyle, D. (June 3, 1988). The meaning of AIDS. *Commonwealth, 115.*

Fisher, J. (1988). Possible effects of reference group-based social influence on AIDS risk behavior and AIDS prevention. *American Psychologist, 11,* 914-920.

Hall, L. (1988). Social work update: Providing culturally relevant mental health services for Central American immigrants. *Hospital and Community Psychiatry, 11,* 1139-1144.

Jacobs, C., & Bowles, D. (Eds.). (1988). *Ethnicity and race: Critical concepts in social work.* Silver Springs, MD: NASW.

Martin, J. (1987). The impact of AIDS on gay male behavior patterns in New York City. *American Journal of Public Health, 77,* 578-581.

McCusick, L., Horstman, W., & Coates, T. (1985). AIDS and sexual behavior reported by gay men in San Francisco. *American Journal of Public Health, 75,* 493-496.

Peterson, J., & Marin, G. (1988). Issues in the prevention of AIDS among black and Hispanic men. *American Psychologist, 11,* 871-877.

Stall, R., Coates, T., & Hoff, C. (1988). Behavior risk reduction for HIV among gay men. *American Psychologist, 11,* 878-885.

Wheeler, D. (June 14, 1989). New studies urged on cultural factors in spread of AIDS. *The Chronicle of Higher Education,* p. A4.

Index

Acculturation, 25,89
  identity development and,
    47-50,58-59
Acoma Pueblo nation, 70
Acquired immune deficiency
    disease. *See* AIDS/HIV
Activist groups, 50,55,88-89,89. *See*
    also GAI (activist group)
AIDS/HIV, 3,36
  epidemiology, 86-88,98
  interventions, 89-94
    Arizona rural population,
      89-91
    Maine rural population,
      97-108
    New York City, 91-94
  literature review, 98-100
  Maine intervention study, 97-108
    follow-up, 104-106
    implementation, 103-104
    needs assessment and
      planning, 101-103
    project description, 101
    service provider implications,
      106-107
  substance abuse and, 87-88
AIDS risk behaviors, 99-103
Alaska Native Sisterhood, 80
Alcohol use/abuse, 100
  condom use and, 105-106
  gay/lesbian literature and, 69-74
Alienation, 57,79
Allegiance, conflicts of, 54-57,70-71
Allen, Paula Gunn, 71-72,78
Alternative gender roles, American
    Indian attitudes toward,
    xviii-xix
Ambivalence, cultural, 70-71

American Indian Community House,
    91
American Indians
  attitudes of
    toward women, 102
    traditional versus acculturated,
      48-49
  birthrate of, 17
  cultural heterogeneity of, 21-22,
    68-69,107
  individuality valued by, xix-xx,11
  religious attitudes of, 7
  romanticized view of, 55,75-76,
    78
  sacred traditions of, xvii-xxiv
  sexuality and, xxi-xxii,16-17
  as term, 68
American Indian Studies Center,
    xvii-xxiv
American Indian Unity Church,
    21-28
Arizona, AIDS/HIV intervention
    program in, 89-91
Attitudes. *See also* Identity
    development
  of American Indians. *See under*
    American Indians
  intrapsychic versus external
    factors in, 61
  religious, xviii-xix, 82
  of service providers, xx-xxi
  traditional versus acculturated
    Indians, 48-49,50
  tribal variations in, 23-28
Aztec, 70

Bars
  gay and lesbian, 71-72. *See also*
    Alcohol use/abuse

Red Power movement, 50
Religious affiliation, 39
Religious attitudes, xvii,xviii-xix,82
    adoption by American Indians, 49
    of American Indians, 7
    of Europeans, 7,17,38
Relocation programs, 39,74-75
Relocation versus social death, 26
Research
    deficit model in, 59-60
    GAI identity model in, 61-62
    on identity development, 45-47
    inadequacy of, 29-30, 44
Role models, 60-61
Role playing, 38
Romanticized view of American
        Indians, 55,75-76,78
Rowell, Ron, 85-95
Rural populations
    AIDS/HIV in
        Arizona, 89-91
        central Maine, 97-108
    as compared with urban, 52-53
Ryan Wylie Care Act, 88

Sacred Being, xvii-xxiv
Sacred traditions of American
        Indians, xvii-xxiv
    colonialism and, xxi-xxii
    mission of, xiii-xxiv
    sacredness of being, xix-xx
    service providers' attitudes
        toward, xx-xxi
    traditional versus contemporary
        views of, xxii-xxiii
Safe sex, 102-106. *See also*
        AIDS/HIV
San Francisco, 15-16,30,31
Sante Fe, New Mexico (poem), 77-78
Self-identity, 45-62, 57. *See also*
        Identity development
    intrapsychic versus external
        factors in, 61
Service delivery implications

    of AIDS education/prevention
        programs, 106-107
    of AIDS/HIV, 85-95
    of gay/lesbian literature, 67-82
    of gender style alternatives, 18
    of identity development, 59-62
    of tribal differences, 25-28
Service providers
    attitudes of, xx-xxi
    deficit model applied by, 59-60
    tribal differences and, 76
Sexism, 12,102
Sexual decision-making, 105-106.
        See also AIDS/HIV
Sexuality
    alternative. *See* Gender
        alternatives
    American Indian view of, xxi-xxii
    bi-, 7-8
    of not men/not women, 12-14
    pan as term, 7-8
    polymorphous perverse as term,
        7-8
Sexually transmitted diseases
        (STDs), 86-87. *See also*
        AIDS/HIV
Sexual play, 7-8
Sexual role playing, 38
Sexual taboos, 8
Sex workers, 93
Sioux nation, 71-72,78
Social control/social ostracism, 52.
        See also Attitudes
Social death, 23-24
Social isolation, 57,79
Social work implications. *See*
        Service delivery
        implications; Service
        providers
Southern Cheyenne nation, 70
Splitting, 52-53
STDs (sexually transmitted
        diseases), 86-87. *See also*
        AIDS/HIV
Steward, Daniel-Harry, 81-82

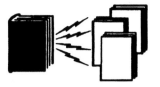

Haworth
DOCUMENT DELIVERY
SERVICE

This valuable service provides a single-article order form for any article from a Haworth journal.

- *Time Saving:* No running around from library to library to find a specific article.
- *Cost Effective:* All costs are kept down to a minimum.
- *Fast Delivery:* Choose from several options, including same-day FAX.
- *No Copyright Hassles:* You will be supplied by the original publisher.
- *Easy Payment:* Choose from several easy payment methods.

Open Accounts Welcome for ...
- Library Interlibrary Loan Departments
- Library Network/Consortia Wishing to Provide Single-Article Services
- Indexing/Abstracting Services with Single Article Provision Services
- Document Provision Brokers and Freelance Information Service Providers

---

MAIL or *FAX* THIS ENTIRE ORDER FORM TO:

Haworth Document Delivery Service
The Haworth Press, Inc.
10 Alice Street
Binghamton, NY 13904-1580

or FAX: 1-800-895-0582
or CALL: 1-800-342-9678
9am-5pm EST

PLEASE SEND ME PHOTOCOPIES OF THE FOLLOWING SINGLE ARTICLES:
1) Journal Title: _____
    Vol/Issue/Year:_____Starting & Ending Pages:_____
Article Title:_____
_____

2) Journal Title: _____
    Vol/Issue/Year:_____Starting & Ending Pages:_____
Article Title:_____
_____

3) Journal Title: _____
    Vol/Issue/Year:_____Starting & Ending Pages:_____
Article Title:_____
_____

4) Journal Title: _____
    Vol/Issue/Year:_____Starting & Ending Pages:_____
Article Title:_____
_____

(See other side for Costs and Payment Information)

COSTS: Please figure your cost to order quality copies of an article.

1. Set-up charge per article: $8.00
   ($8.00 × number of separate articles) _____

2. Photocopying charge for each article:

   1-10 pages: $1.00 _____

   11-19 pages: $3.00 _____

   20-29 pages: $5.00 _____

   30+ pages: $2.00/10 pages _____

3. Flexicover (optional): $2.00/article _____

4. Postage & Handling: US: $1.00 for the first article/

   $.50 each additional article _____

   Federal Express: $25.00 _____

   Outside US: $2.00 for first article/

   $.50 each additional article _____

5. Same-day FAX service: $.35 per page _____

GRAND TOTAL: _____

METHOD OF PAYMENT: (please check one)

❑ Check enclosed   ❑ Please ship and bill. PO # _____
(sorry we can ship and bill to bookstores only! All others must pre-pay)

❑ Charge to my credit card: ❑ Visa; ❑ MasterCard; ❑ Discover;
❑ American Express;

Account Number: _____ Expiration date: _____

Signature: ✗ _____

Name: _____ Institution: _____

Address: _____

_____

City: _____ State: _____ Zip: _____

Phone Number: _____ FAX Number: _____

MAIL or *FAX* THIS ENTIRE ORDER FORM TO:

Haworth Document Delivery Service
The Haworth Press, Inc.
10 Alice Street
Binghamton, NY 13904-1580

or FAX: 1-800-895-0582
or CALL: 1-800-342-9678
9am-5pm EST)

 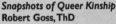